HEALTHY EATING ONE-POT COOKBOOK

Healthy Eating
ONE-POT Cookbook

101 Effortless Meals for Your
Instant Pot™, Sheet Pan,
Skillet, and Dutch Oven

LAUREN KEATING

Photography by Nadine Greeff

ROCKRIDGE
PRESS

Interior and Cover Designer: Merideth Harte
Photo Art Director: Sue Smith
Editor: Kim Suarez
Production Editor: Andrew Yackira
Photography © 2018 Nadine Greeff
Illustrations: Merideth Harte

ISBN: Print 978-1-64152-347-9 | eBook 978-1-64152-348-6

To my family, for teaching
me that no goal is too big to
pursue and encouraging me
always to follow my dreams.

CONTENTS

HEALTHY EATING, ONE POT AT A TIME

I've always felt that if food isn't delicious, it isn't worth eating. Healthy eating doesn't mean going on fad diets—or even following a strict diet at all. It's about focusing on deliciously satisfying foods that nourish your body and soul—and making them a priority. That's what this book focuses on. It's not a diet book; it's a book featuring healthy, flavorful, one-pot recipes so you don't have to go "on a diet" ever again just to eat healthy.

The Golden Principles of Healthy Eating

So, what is healthy eating? For starters, it means focusing on fresh, whole foods with an emphasis on fruits and vegetables, often referred to as clean eating. It also means choosing unrefined whole grains, such as whole-wheat flour, brown rice, and oats, over more processed options.

For the most part, this book relies on food that comes from the grocery store's perimeter and is sold without a label. When you do venture into those inner aisles for items such as canned beans, packaged chicken stock, or spices, be sure to check the labels. Avoid chemicals and artificial flavors, and monitor for salt and added sugars.

Buy the best quality food you can easily afford—it tastes better and is less likely to have unnecessary additives and fillers. When it makes sense, look for organic produce (see the Dirty Dozen and Clean Fifteen™, page 145) and buy meat, dairy, and eggs from sustainable and local sources whose animals are raised humanely and without antibiotics, growth hormones, and other unnecessary restrictions such as being caged.

The Logistical Challenge

When you make the commitment to healthier eating habits, you'll naturally want more control over the quality of the food you eat. That's difficult when you're relying on other people to prepare your food, whether it's in the form of take-out meals or even prepared items from the grocery store. Prepared healthy, clean-eating options can be found, but they tend to be expensive.

The best and most cost-effective way to eat healthy is to make your own meals at home from whole, fresh ingredients. I get how challenging that can seem. We're all busy; we get home late, and we're tired. Throw in homework, laundry, after-school or after-work activities and who has the time to cook? Just the idea of cooking can be overwhelming—not to mention that endless pile of dishes that needs to be washed when you're done.

Even though logistical challenges exist, healthy eating should be a priority. Along with physical activity, it's crucial to maintaining your physical and mental health. When I eat well, I feel better—and I have more energy. And I'm here to help.

The One-Pot Solution

Cooking dinner used to be the last thing I felt like doing after a long day. But once I discovered the beauty of one-pot cooking, my nightly routine was transformed. Now, instead of being tempted by take-out, I know a homemade meal made with nutritious ingredients is just a few minutes away. Plus, as there's only one pot, cleanup is a breeze!

People have been making one-pot meals on their stovetops and in their ovens for decades, but modern kitchen appliances such as electric pressure cookers, slow cookers, and air fryers make one-pot cooking easier—and healthier—than ever.

In this cookbook, you'll find some of my go-to favorites for easy, healthy weeknight recipes. Many also make delicious leftovers for lunch the next day. And, because dinner isn't the only meal people eat, I've included recipes for breakfast and dessert.

Whether you already embrace clean eating as part of your healthy lifestyle or need some inspiration to increase the use of whole foods in your diet, I hope these recipes motivate you into the kitchen and get you excited about cooking and eating in a more healthy and satisifying way.

Chapter 1

HEALTHY EATING MADE EASY

I'VE BEEN FOCUSED ON HEALTHY EATING FOR a long time now, so I have a few tricks up my sleeve. In this chapter, I cover the basics and also let you in on some of my favorite cooking and meal planning tips—from helpful hints on what ingredients to keep in your kitchen and which ones to avoid to fast prep solutions that will help you get meals on the table quickly. You'll also learn my five tricks to help you keep your portion sizes under control without feeling deprived. My approach to fuss-free weeknight cooking makes healthy eating a breeze—oh, and have I mentioned delicious? With these tips and some new one-pot recipes up your sleeve, you'll be a pro in no time.

What to Eat

Clean eating doesn't mean you have to live off salads or that you can never eat dessert. It's about focusing on real, minimally processed foods without added chemicals and cooking them in a way that uses healthy fats, herbs, and spices for a flavor boost. With that in mind, I've noted foods to enjoy to their fullest, those to limit to special occasions or enjoy in moderation, and foods to avoid when possible.

ENJOY

One of the best things about practicing clean eating is that you can enjoy most minimally processed, whole foods without limitation and without worrying about things like counting calories or tracking every bite you take. Bulk up your meals with ingredients like fresh fruits and vegetables; lean proteins such as fish, beans, and eggs; and nuts and seeds. You can also use herbs and spices, both fresh and dried, to add tons of flavor to your meals. If it doesn't have an ingredient label or you can grow it in your garden, it likely belongs in this category. These ingredients should fill the majority of your plate. Additionally, try to incorporate them into your desserts and snacks as often as you can.

LIMIT

Some foods are okay in moderation, but, even though they're generally healthy, they can quickly add a lot of calories to your plate if you aren't careful. For the best success, limit sugars, including natural sugars such as honey and pure maple syrup, healthy fats such as olive oil, avocado, and tahini, whole grains like brown rice and farro, and starchy vegetables like potatoes. Dairy and processed meats such as sausage or bacon also fall under this category, and always look for versions without added sugar, nitrates, or other additives. Use these ingredients to add a pop of flavor to your plate, but approach them as a treat to be enjoyed in small amounts.

AVOID

I'm not generally a fan of strict food rules or declaring certain foods off limits, but for long-term results, people who follow a clean-eating way of life should avoid some foods completely. This includes highly processed snacks and convenience food such as French fries and chips, commercially prepared cookies and pastries, and sugary drinks. You should also avoid artificial sweeteners—besides not having any nutritional value, studies have shown they can actually lead to overeating!

Also be careful with low-fat and nonfat foods and check labels carefully. Some, like most fat-free Greek yogurts, are okay, but others are loaded with extra sugars and artificial ingredients to make up for the flavor and texture lost when removing the fat.

HOW MUCH FOOD? A LOW-STRESS GUIDE TO PORTION CONTROL

- **Use a small plate.** Ditch the dinner plate and use a salad plate instead. We eat with our eyes, and having a smaller plate that's filled with food can seem more satisfying than the same amount of food presented on a larger plate.
- **Fill up with veggies.** Vegetables are a healthy way to bulk up your meals, with their water and fiber content helping you feel full. Fill half your plate with vegetables or add a small side salad to your meal. You can also add fruits and vegetables to desserts. Try my Chocolate Zucchini Cake (page 112).
- **Drink water.** It's easy to mistake thirst for hunger. Make sure you're drinking plenty of water, both with your meals and throughout the day, to stay satisfied. Aim for ½ to 1 ounce of water per pound of body weight per day.
- **Keep the leftovers in the kitchen.** Instead of bringing everything to the table and eating family style, fix your plate in the kitchen and leave the leftovers there. That way, you'll be less likely to have "just a little more."
- **Eat mindfully.** Speaking of the table . . . eat there, not on the couch in front of the TV. You'll be able to focus on enjoying your food without distraction and won't accidentally finish everything on your plate without even realizing it—or tasting it.

Fast Prep Solutions

The key to no-fuss cooking is all about being prepared. Here are some tips to help you prepare healthy recipes in a snap.

Meal plan: Spending a few minutes creating a plan for the week means no wasted time standing in front of the refrigerator wondering what to make and no extra trips to the grocery store for random ingredients you might not have.

Batch cook: Double or even triple recipes for pantry staples such as beans, rice and other grains, sauces, and stocks. They'll keep in the refrigerator for a few days or frozen for longer-term storage. That way, you'll have them ready to go when you need them.

Embrace leftovers: Cook once and eat twice! Make extra for dinner and enjoy leftovers for lunch the next day, or dinner again later in the week. You can also reimagine leftovers so you don't get bored—enjoy Ratatouille (page 125) as a side dish one night, then add it to pasta the next.

Toss your peeler: There's no need to spend time peeling soft-skinned vegetables such as carrots, potatoes, or zucchini—just be sure to wash them well before cooking. And don't worry about getting the perfect dice; just chop veggies to roughly the same size so they cook at the same pace.

Plan ahead: Mornings can be rushed, so I chop vegetables and measure any other ingredients for slow cooker meals the previous night. The next morning, you only need to pull them out of the refrigerator, put them in the slow cooker, and turn it on!

Refrigerator and Pantry Staples

Stocking your kitchen with healthy foods, so everything is within easy reach and you're not tempted by those chips or cookies, is one of the most important things you can do to set yourself up for weeknight cooking success. Following are some general ideas, but be sure to adapt them to your personal tastes—it doesn't matter how much broccoli you have; if you don't like it, you'll never eat it.

THE REFRIGERATOR
Citrus fruits: Lemons and limes can be used in simple dressings and marinades and are an easy way to perk up flavors.

PERFECT PAIRINGS

The recipes in this book have been designed to stand on their own, but some do go together well for a more rounded meal, or if you're serving guests. Here are some ideas to get you started.

Recipe 1 pairs well with . . .	Recipe 2	Prep Tip
Italian Eggplant Stacks (page 36)	Salad with All-Purpose Greek Dressing (page 137)	Make a double batch of dressing while the eggplant bakes (it's nice to have extra on hand); make a salad with romaine lettuce hearts, cucumbers, tomatoes, and peperoncini.
Lighter Falafel (page 35)	Baba Ghanoush (page 121)	Make the baba ghanoush a day ahead so it can chill. It will keep, refrigerated in an airtight container, for several days.
Baked Sausage Risotto (page 75)	Roasted Brussels Sprouts with Bacon & Pecans (page 127)	Bake two recipes at the same time. Adjust your oven racks so both your Dutch oven and sheet pan fit.
Oven-Roasted Tandoori Chicken Thighs (page 67)	Pressure Cooker Brown Rice (page 124)	Start the rice and then put the chicken in the oven. They'll be ready to eat at the same time.
Lamb Meat Pies (see Air-Fried Lamb Meat Pies, page 78)	Ratatouille (page 125)	Instead of cooking the meat pies in the air fryer, place them on a sheet pan and bake them alongside the ratatouille; they'll take about 45 minutes.

Fat-free Greek yogurt: Besides being an easy grab-and-go breakfast, you can use yogurt as a marinade for chicken or swirl it into soups and stews to add a creamy element or tone down spiciness.

Fresh herbs: Herbs such as cilantro and basil add tons of instant flavor to simple recipes.

Green vegetables: Ingredients such as broccoli, zucchini, and bell peppers are a great starting place for most meals and mean a quick stir-fry is never far away.

Hard cheese: Hard cheeses such as Parmesan and aged Cheddar last a long time, and it only takes a little to add loads of flavor to your food.

Lean proteins: Quick-cooking lean proteins such as skinless chicken breast, shrimp, and eggs can be combined with other kitchen staples to create endless meal options.

Pizza dough: Pizza is delicious, but pizza dough can be used for so much more—bake it into rolls to go with soup, use it to make a meat pie, or turn it into cinnamon buns.

THE PANTRY

Canned tomatoes: Canned no-salt-added tomatoes are great in soups and stews, or for making a quick pasta sauce. I prefer fire-roasted varieties, which also add a subtle smoky element.

Dried herbs and spices: Pick one or two of your favorite international flavor profiles and stock up. Having a variety of dried herbs and spices means you can make anything from Indian curries to Italian soups, even when fresh are not available.

Garlic and onions: Almost every recipe I make starts with at least one of these ingredients. I stock up every time I go to the grocery store.

Stock: I usually have homemade chicken and vegetable stock (see pages 133 and 135) in my freezer, but I always keep a few cartons of low-sodium stock in the cabinet as backup. Use it to make a quick soup or add extra flavor to a pot of whole grains.

Whole grains: Rice, farro, and quinoa can form the base for many meals. Each has its own unique flavor, so I always have a good variety on hand to choose from.

One-Pot Cooking

I hate recipes touted as "one pot" when they really aren't. You won't find any of those in this book. You might need a mixing bowl or a whisk here or there, but each recipe requires only one piece of cooking equipment, as listed following. They're perfect for busy weeknights because they only take a few minutes of prep work, and cooking everything together means fewer dishes to wash when dinner is over.

AIR FRYER
These countertop ovens use a fan to circulate air around food as it cooks, mimicking the crispy texture that frying provides without a ton of oil. It's important not to crowd your food, so look for a larger model. Otherwise, you'll have to cook in batches.

DUTCH OVEN
These heavy, lidded pots, usually made from enamel-coated cast iron, can be used on the stovetop and in the oven.

ELECTRIC PRESSURE COOKER
Pressure cookers let you make things that would normally take a long time in, usually, under 1 hour. Modern versions also let you brown meat or vegetables right in the same pot. A 6-quart pot is big enough to handle 4 to 6 servings of most foods.

SHEET PAN
These flat pans are used in the oven. Look for those with a short rim around the edge to keep wet ingredients from spilling off.

SKILLET
Skillets are typically used for stovetop cooking, but many can also be used in the oven. For one-pot meals, you'll want a big one!

SLOW COOKER
I think of slow cookers as the opposite of pressure cookers. They're perfect for stews and big cuts of meat that cook all day to tender, tasty perfection with minimal attention.

Chapter 2

BREAKFAST

CARROT CAKE OATMEAL

Prep time: 5 minutes / **Time to pressure:** 5 minutes / **Cook time:** 4 minutes / **Release time:** 15 minutes

This recipe turns one of my favorite desserts—carrot cake—into a nutritious breakfast. Steel cut oats take only a few minutes to cook when you use a pressure cooker, and they turn out really creamy. I add shredded carrots to the oats while they cook, then stir in classic carrot cake flavors such as raisins, nuts, and coconut. **Serves 4**

2 cups gluten-free steel cut oats

8 carrots, shredded

½ cup raisins

½ cup unsweetened shredded coconut

¼ cup chopped pecans

2 teaspoons vanilla extract

2 teaspoons lemon zest

1 teaspoon ground cinnamon

¼ teaspoon Celtic sea salt or kosher salt

4 tablespoons maple syrup

1. In your pressure cooker, combine 4 cups of water, the oats, and carrots. Lock the lid in place and set the cooker to High pressure for 4 minutes.

2. When the cook time ends, let the pressure release naturally for 15 minutes; manually release any remaining pressure.

3. Carefully remove the lid and stir in the raisins, coconut, pecans, vanilla, lemon zest, cinnamon, and salt.

4. Drizzle 1 tablespoon of maple syrup over each serving.

Leftovers tip: Oatmeal is great reheated on the stovetop or microwave, so I like to make a big batch and eat it over the course of the week. It thickens while it sits, so add a splash of nut milk or water to loosen it up when reheating.

Per Serving: Calories: 329; Total Fat: 10g; Saturated Fat: 6g; Protein: 6g; Total Carbs: 58g; Fiber: 9g; Net Carbs: 49g; Cholesterol: 0mg

DAIRY-FREE, GLUTEN-FREE, VEGAN, VEGETARIAN

EGGS IN PURGATORY

Prep time: 5 minutes / **Cook time:** 20 minutes

Eggs in purgatory is an Italian-style breakfast consisting of eggs poached in a spicy tomato sauce. It's usually made for breakfast or brunch, but it's the kind of warm, comforting food that we also love to eat for dinner on snowy nights. I stir baby spinach into the sauce while it cooks—it has a mild flavor that goes well with the dish and is a great way to add extra vegetables. **Serves 4**

2 tablespoons extra-virgin
olive oil

6 garlic cloves, minced

4 cups fresh baby spinach

4 cups Super Simple Marinara
(page 132)

2 teaspoons red pepper flakes

8 large eggs

2 tablespoons chopped
fresh parsley

1 whole-grain baguette,
for serving

1. Preheat the oven to 350°F.

2. In a large ovenproof skillet over medium heat, heat the olive oil.

3. Add the garlic. Cook for 2 to 3 minutes until fragrant. Stir in the spinach, marinara, and red pepper flakes. Cook for 2 to 4 minutes, or until the spinach wilts.

4. Using a spoon, create 8 small wells in the sauce. Crack 1 egg into each well. Transfer the skillet to the oven. Bake for 10 to 12 minutes until the eggs are set.

5. Sprinkle with the parsley and serve with the baguette.

Substitution tip: Instead of spinach, add 2 cups of Ratatouille (page 125) to the sauce.

Per Serving: Calories: 409; Total Fat: 19g; Saturated Fat: 5g; Protein: 23g; Total Carbs: 41g; Fiber: 8g; Net Carbs: 33g; Cholesterol: 372mg

DAIRY-FREE, NUT-FREE, VEGETARIAN

SWEET POTATO BREAKFAST BOWLS

Prep time: 5 minutes / **Time to pressure:** 5 minutes / **Cook time:** 8 minutes / **Release time:** 5 minutes

A bowl of warm mashed sweet potatoes is a nice alternative to porridge for breakfast. Coconut milk and a splash of vanilla highlight the potatoes' natural sweetness, so they don't need any additional sugar. I love the contrast of tart blueberries against the sweet potatoes, but you can use your favorite berries, or top your bowl with sliced bananas. **Serves 6**

5 medium sweet potatoes, peeled and diced

½ cup canned full-fat coconut milk

1 teaspoon vanilla extract

1½ cups fresh blueberries, or frozen and thawed

1 teaspoon ground cinnamon

1. In your pressure cooker, combine the sweet potatoes and 1 cup of water. Lock the lid in place and set the cooker to High pressure for 8 minutes.

2. When the cook time ends, manually release the pressure.

3. Carefully remove the lid and add the coconut milk and vanilla. Using a large spoon, stir or mash the potatoes until creamy.

4. Top each serving with ¼ cup of blueberries and a sprinkle of cinnamon.

Substitution tip: If you don't have a pressure cooker, cook the potatoes in a slow cooker for 4 hours on high heat.

Per Serving: Calories: 163; Total Fat: 5g; Saturated Fat: 4g; Protein: 3g; Total Carbs: 29g; Fiber: 5g; Net Carbs: 24g; Cholesterol: 0mg

DAIRY-FREE, GLUTEN-FREE, VEGAN, VEGETARIAN

APPLE CINNAMON BUNS

Prep time: 15 minutes / **Cook time:** 15 minutes

Who doesn't love cinnamon buns? I gave these buns a makeover by adding shredded apple and cutting back on the cinnamon-sugar filling for a breakfast that's tasty enough to double as dessert. Cooking them in an air fryer cuts down on baking time and turns out buns that are slightly crisp on the outside, but warm and fluffy on the inside. **Serves 6**

10 ounces Pizza Dough (page 141), or store-bought whole-wheat dough

All-purpose or white whole-wheat flour, for preparing the work surface

1 tablespoon cold unsalted butter

2 apples, cored

1 tablespoon ground cinnamon

1 tablespoon sugar

¼ teaspoon Celtic sea salt or kosher salt

1. Remove the dough from the refrigerator 5 to 10 minutes before you plan to use it, to take the chill off.

2. Lightly flour a work surface. Using a rolling pin, roll the dough into a 12-by-8-inch rectangle. Grate the butter into an even layer covering the dough; repeat with the apples. Sprinkle evenly with the cinnamon, sugar, and salt.

3. Starting at one of the long sides, tightly roll the dough into a cylinder. Slice the cylinder crosswise into 6 rounds.

4. Place the buns in your air fryer's basket. Fry at 325°F for 12 to 15 minutes, or until the tops are golden and the dough is cooked through.

Substitution tip: Instead of apples and cinnamon, give these rolls a springtime feel with raspberries and chopped almonds.

Per Serving: Calories: 226; Total Fat: 5g; Saturated Fat: 1g; Protein: 6g; Total Carbs: 45g; Fiber: 5g; Net Carbs: 40g; Cholesterol: 5mg

NUT-FREE, VEGETARIAN

SMOKED SALMON FRITTATA

Prep time: 10 minutes / **Cook time:** 20 minutes

I love frittatas! Think of this egg-based dish like a crustless quiche—it's started on the stovetop and finished in the oven, so you don't need to worry about folding or flipping like you would with an omelet. This Scandinavian-inspired version is stuffed with potatoes and smoked salmon and topped with fresh dill for something a little off the beaten path. **Serves 4**

1 tablespoon extra-virgin olive oil

1 russet potato, diced

1 onion, diced

¼ cup Garden Vegetable Stock (page 135), or store-bought low-sodium vegetable stock

4 large eggs

2 large egg whites

2 tablespoons fat-free plain Greek yogurt

2 ounces smoked salmon, chopped

1 tablespoon fresh dill, chopped

1. Preheat the oven to 450°F.

2. In an ovenproof skillet over medium-high heat, heat the olive oil.

3. Add the potato and onion. Cook for 5 minutes until the onion softens and the potato begins to brown.

4. Pour in the vegetable stock. Simmer for about 5 minutes until the potatoes are cooked and the liquid is absorbed.

5. In a medium bowl, whisk the eggs, egg whites, and yogurt to combine. Pour the egg mixture into the skillet. Top evenly with the salmon. Bake for 8 to 10 minutes, or until the frittata is lightly browned and fluffy. Top with the dill.

Ingredient tip: It's easy to confuse smoked salmon and lox, but they aren't the same. Smoked salmon is cured or brined before being cold smoked for added flavor. Lox is brined but not smoked.

Per Serving: Calories: 186; Total Fat: 9g; Saturated Fat: 2g; Protein: 13g; Total Carbs: 14g; Fiber: 1g; Net Carbs: 13g; Cholesterol: 189mg

GLUTEN-FREE, NUT-FREE

SWEET POTATO "EGG IN A HOLE"

Prep time: 5 minutes / **Cook time:** 20 minutes

I resisted the sweet potato toast trend for a long time, but eventually gave in—and, it turns out, people were really onto something! Sweet potato planks are crisp on the outside, tender on the inside, and pair surprisingly well with classic toast toppings—from butter to peanut butter to avocado. This version is an homage to one of my favorite childhood breakfasts, egg in a hole. **Serves 4**

1 large sweet potato, cut lengthwise into 4 (¼-inch-thick) planks

1 tablespoon extra-virgin olive oil

4 large eggs

Celtic sea salt or kosher salt

Freshly ground black pepper

1. Preheat the oven to 450°F.

2. Using a 3-inch round cookie cutter or sharp knife, cut a hole in the center of each sweet potato plank. Brush both sides of the potatoes with olive oil and arrange them on a sheet pan. Bake for 15 minutes, or until the bottoms begin to caramelize.

3. Flip the potatoes. Crack 1 egg into each hole. Bake for 5 minutes more, or until the eggs are set. Season to taste with salt and pepper.

Variation tip: Use this same technique to make "traditional" sweet potato toast, too. Skip cutting the hole and, after the toast is cooked, top it with anything from peanut butter and banana slices to avocado and smoked salmon.

Per Serving: Calories: 129; Total Fat: 9g; Saturated Fat: 2g; Protein: 7g; Total Carbs: 7g; Fiber: 1g; Net Carbs: 6g; Cholesterol: 88mg

DAIRY-FREE, GLUTEN-FREE, NUT-FREE, VEGETARIAN

DUTCH BABY PANCAKE WITH SLICED STRAWBERRIES

Prep time: 10 minutes / **Cook time:** 25 minutes

Dutch babies are giant baked pancakes that are served in slices. They puff up like a soufflé, so they're really impressive when they first come out of the oven. *Serves 4*

1 pint fresh strawberries, trimmed and sliced

3 tablespoons plus 1 teaspoon sugar, divided

3 large eggs

⅔ cup milk

Zest of 1 lemon

¼ teaspoon Celtic sea salt or kosher salt

⅔ cup white whole-wheat flour

1 tablespoon unsalted butter

2 tablespoons sliced almonds

Maple syrup, for serving (optional)

1. Preheat the oven to 400°F.

2. In a small bowl, stir together the strawberries and 1 teaspoon of sugar. Set aside.

3. In a large bowl, whisk the eggs and milk until smooth. Add the lemon zest, remaining 3 tablespoons of sugar, and salt. Whisk to combine, then slowly mix in the flour to form a thin, smooth batter.

4. Place the butter in a 9-inch ovenproof skillet and put the skillet in the oven for 2 to 3 minutes, or until the butter melts. Swirl the skillet to coat it with melted butter. Pour the batter into the skillet.

5. Return the pan to the oven and bake for 20 minutes, or until the Dutch baby is puffed and golden brown. Remove from the oven and let cool for a few minutes—the pancake will deflate as it cools.

6. Top the Dutch baby with the strawberries and almonds. Serve with maple syrup (if using).

Substitution tip: If you don't have maple syrup, this Dutch baby is also delicious drizzled with honey or dusted with powdered sugar.

Per Serving: Calories: 250; Total Fat: 10g; Saturated Fat: 4g; Protein: 10g; Total Carbs: 34g; Fiber: 5g; Net Carbs: 29g; Cholesterol: 150mg

VEGETARIAN

GOOD MORNING GRANOLA

Prep time: 5 minutes / **Cook time:** 20 minutes

This homemade granola is better than anything you can find in the store. Egg white helps form big, crispy chunks while lemon zest gives the granola a bright, sunny flavor. I love stirring dried cranberries into mine, but you can substitute any dried berries or raisins. Enjoy it straight from the pan, in a bowl with milk, or sprinkled on top of yogurt. **Serves 6**

2½ cups rolled oats

½ cup maple syrup

½ cup chopped walnuts

¼ cup unsweetened shredded coconut

1 large egg white, beaten

¼ cup chia or hemp seeds, or a combination

Zest of 1 lemon

Pinch Celtic sea salt

½ cup dried cranberries (reduced-sugar if you can find them)

1. Preheat the oven to 300°F.

2. In a large bowl, combine the oats, maple syrup, walnuts, coconut, egg white, and seeds. Stir until thoroughly combined. Pour onto a sheet pan. Bake for 20 minutes.

3. Stir in the lemon zest, salt, and cranberries.

Ingredient tip: Egg white helps the granola stick together in big, crunchy clumps. For a vegan version of this granola, simply leave it out. The granola will be a little looser, but the flavor will be the same.

Per Serving: Calories: 237; Total Fat: 9g; Saturated Fat: 2g; Protein: 7g; Total Carbs: 33g; Fiber: 3g; Net Carbs: 30g; Cholesterol: 0mg

DAIRY-FREE, GLUTEN-FREE, VEGETARIAN

SHEET PAN BACON & EGGS

Prep time: 10 minutes / **Cook time:** 30 minutes

We used to go to the diner every Saturday morning after the gym, and I'd order bacon, eggs, and potatoes—every week. It didn't take long for me to realize I could make it better and cheaper at home. This breakfast is all cooked together on one sheet pan, so there's only one pan to wash. It couldn't be easier! **Serves 4**

8 sugar-free bacon slices

1 russet potato, diced

½ green bell pepper, seeded and diced

½ onion, diced

1 tablespoon extra-virgin olive oil

1 teaspoon dried parsley

Celtic sea salt or kosher salt

Freshly ground black pepper

8 large eggs

1. Preheat the oven to 400°F. Line a sheet pan with parchment paper.

2. Arrange the bacon in a single layer on half of the prepared sheet pan. Spread the potato, green bell pepper, and onion on the other side. Drizzle the potatoes with the olive oil and season with the parsley, salt, and pepper. Bake for 20 minutes. Stir the vegetables.

3. Crack the eggs over the potatoes. Bake for 8 to 10 minutes more until the eggs are cooked to your liking. Season to taste with salt and pepper.

Substitution tip: If you don't feel like bacon, use breakfast sausage. Or skip the meat entirely for a vegetarian breakfast.

Per Serving: Calories: 431; Total Fat: 29g; Saturated Fat: 9g; Protein: 28g; Total Carbs: 13g; Fiber: 1g; Net Carbs: 12g; Cholesterol: 414mg

DAIRY-FREE, GLUTEN-FREE, NUT-FREE

AIR-FRIED STUFFED APPLES

Prep time: 10 minutes / **Cook time:** 13 minutes

When I was a kid, I always thought the best part of camping was making apples in the campfire. We'd stuff them with oats, cinnamon sugar, and butter, wrap them in aluminum foil, and let them roast until they were soft and the filling was syrupy.

This air-fried version means you can enjoy stuffed apples year-round. I add pecans for some crunch and just a touch of maple syrup for a hint of sweetness. **Serves 4**

4 apples

1 teaspoon ground cinnamon

¼ cup rolled oats

2 tablespoons chopped pecans

Pinch Celtic sea salt or kosher salt

½ teaspoon maple syrup

2 teaspoons unsalted butter

1. Slice the top off each apple. Using a paring knife, remove the core, being careful not to cut all the way through the bottom of the apples. Sprinkle the inside of the apples with the cinnamon.

2. In a small bowl, stir together the oats, pecans, and salt. Divide the filling among the apples. Drizzle with the syrup and top each apple with ½ teaspoon of butter.

3. Arrange the apples in your air fryer's basket. Fry at 350°F for 13 minutes.

Ingredient tip: Gala apples are my favorite variety to use for these baked apples—they're naturally sweet and crisp, so they hold their shape well when cooked.

Per Serving: Calories: 152; Total Fat: 3g; Saturated Fat: 1g; Protein: 1g; Total Carbs: 34g; Fiber: 6g; Net Carbs: 28g; Cholesterol: 5mg

GLUTEN-FREE, VEGETARIAN

SAUSAGE & EGG SCRAMBLE

Prep time: 5 minutes / **Cook time:** 15 minutes

This skillet breakfast is really easy, so it's one I make often. Mixing in slices of breakfast sausage infuses tons of flavor into each bite and helps stretch the sausage further than serving it on the side. Cooking the eggs over lower heat and stirring constantly gives them a soft, creamy texture and keeps them from drying out. **Serves 4**

1 tablespoon extra-virgin
   olive oil

1 onion, chopped

1 bell pepper, any
   color, chopped

2 breakfast sausage
   links, sliced

6 large eggs, beaten

2 cups fresh baby spinach

1. In a large skillet over medium heat, heat the olive oil.

2. Add the onion and bell pepper. Cook for 3 to 5 minutes, or until softened.

3. Add the sausage. Cook for 3 to 4 minutes to brown.

4. Whisk in the eggs. Cook for 3 to 4 minutes, stirring constantly, until the eggs are set but still creamy.

5. Add the spinach, stirring until wilted.

Substitution tip: For a vegetarian version, omit the sausage and add 1 cup of sliced mushrooms instead.

Per Serving: Calories: 183; Total Fat: 13g; Saturated Fat: 3g; Protein: 12g; Total Carbs: 6g; Fiber: 1g; Net Carbs: 5g; Cholesterol: 284mg

DAIRY-FREE, GLUTEN-FREE, NUT-FREE

BUTTERNUT SQUASH HASH & EGGS

Prep time: 10 minutes / **Cook time:** 25 minutes

This is one of my all-time favorite breakfasts—I make it every fall when butternut squash comes into season. To play off the fall theme, I use apple cider as my cooking liquid instead of water. It gives the hash a subtle sweetness and the apple flavor goes really nicely with the squash and chard. If you don't have cider on hand, apple juice also works. **Serves 4**

1 tablespoon extra-virgin olive oil

1 onion, diced

2 garlic cloves, minced

1 butternut squash (about 2 pounds), peeled and diced

1 red potato, diced

½ cup apple cider

1 cup chopped Swiss chard

4 large eggs

2 tablespoons fresh oregano leaves

Celtic sea salt or kosher salt

Freshly ground black pepper

1. Preheat the oven to 400°F.

2. In a large ovenproof skillet over medium-high heat, heat the olive oil.

3. Add the onion and garlic. Cook for 3 or 4 minutes until softened.

4. Add the squash, red potato, and cider. Simmer for 10 minutes, or until the vegetables are soft and the cider is absorbed.

5. Stir in the chard. Using a spoon, create 4 wells in the hash. Crack 1 egg into each well. Transfer the skillet to the oven and bake for 10 minutes, or until the eggs are set.

6. Sprinkle with the oregano and season to taste with salt and pepper.

Make-ahead tip: To make this dish ahead, stop after stirring in the chard in step 5, and serve the hash with Pressure-Cooked Hard-boiled Eggs (page 138).

Per Serving: Calories: 277; Total Fat: 9g; Saturated Fat: 2g; Protein: 10g; Total Carbs: 44g; Fiber: 7g; Net Carbs: 37g; Cholesterol: 186mg

DAIRY-FREE, GLUTEN-FREE, NUT-FREE, VEGETARIAN

MIXED BERRY FRENCH TOAST CASSEROLE

Prep time: 15 minutes / **Cook time:** 40 minutes

French toast casserole is great when you need to serve breakfast to a crowd—instead of making French toast slice by slice, it all cooks together in a Dutch oven. The top comes out crispy while the inside is soft and fluffy—almost like bread pudding. Traditional recipes use sweetened condensed milk and corn syrup, but I lighten things up by using coconut milk and maple syrup instead. **Serves 6**

---

8 large egg whites

1½ cups lite coconut milk

¼ cup maple syrup, plus more for serving (optional)

1 teaspoon vanilla extract

2 teaspoons ground cinnamon

12 slices whole-wheat bread, cut into 1-inch cubes (about 6 cups)

2 cups mixed fresh berries, such as strawberries and blueberries

1. Preheat the oven to 350°F.

2. In a large bowl, whisk the egg whites, coconut milk, maple syrup, vanilla, and cinnamon until well combined.

3. Put the bread cubes in your Dutch oven. Pour the liquid ingredients over the bread. Stir well to combine. Mix in the berries. Let sit for 10 minutes.

4. Bake, uncovered, for 30 to 40 minutes until all the liquid is absorbed and the casserole's top is lightly browned and crispy.

5. Remove from the oven and let cool for 5 minutes. Serve with additional syrup (if using).

Make-ahead tip: Complete steps 1 through 3 the night before and let the bread soak in the refrigerator overnight, covered. Place the pan on the counter while the oven heats to take the chill off before baking as directed.

Per Serving: Calories: 227; Total Fat: 3g; Saturated Fat: 1g; Protein: 13g; Total Carbs: 38g; Fiber: 5g; Net Carbs: 33g; Cholesterol: 0mg

---

DAIRY-FREE, VEGETARIAN

BANANA BREAD

Prep time: 10 minutes / **Time to pressure:** 5 minutes / **Cook time:** 1 hour 15 minutes / **Release time:** 5 minutes

Why bake banana bread in the pressure cooker? Besides the fact that you can and it's always fun to try something new, it comes out perfect and it doesn't heat up the house. The bread steams instead of bakes, resulting in moist bread with small, tightly packed crumbs. Don't skip the paper towel and aluminum foil. It seems strange, but it helps trap moisture and ensures the bread comes out beautifully browned on top and not soggy. **Serves 4**

Nonstick cooking spray, for preparing the cake pan

¼ cup packed light brown sugar

¼ cup granulated sugar

1 large egg

½ cup fat-free plain Greek yogurt

½ teaspoon vanilla extract

1 cup plus 1 tablespoon white whole-wheat flour

½ teaspoon baking soda

¼ teaspoon Celtic sea salt or kosher salt

2 very ripe bananas, peeled

¼ cup chopped walnuts

1. Coat a 6-inch cake pan with cooking spray and set aside.

2. In a large bowl, whisk the brown and granulated sugars and egg until smooth.

3. Stir in the yogurt and vanilla.

4. Gently stir in the flour, baking soda, and salt to form a very thick batter.

5. Add the bananas. Using a heavy spoon, mash the bananas against the side of the bowl and stir them into the batter. Fold in the walnuts. Pour the batter into the prepared pan. Cover it loosely with a paper towel and wrap the whole pan in foil.

6. Place a wire rack in the bottom of your pressure cooker. Pour in 1 cup of water. Place the cake pan on top of the rack. Lock the lid in place and set the cooker to High pressure for 1 hour and 15 minutes.

7. When the cook time ends, manually release the pressure.

8. Carefully remove the lid and the bread. Let the bread cool before unwrapping.

Substitution tip: I love the classic banana-walnut combination, but use any nuts you prefer. Try pecans or satisfy your sweet tooth by adding dark chocolate chips.

Per Serving: Calories: 325; Total Fat: 3g; Saturated Fat: 1g; Protein: 19g; Total Carbs: 66g; Fiber: 3g; Net Carbs: 63g; Cholesterol: 47mg

---

VEGETARIAN

PEACHES & CREAM QUINOA BOWLS

Prep time: 5 minutes / **Time to pressure:** 10 minutes / **Cook time:** 1 minute / **Release time:** 10 minutes

Quinoa is nice for a change of pace when you want a warm breakfast but are tired of oats or eggs. Cooking it in coconut milk with peaches and vanilla results in a sweet, creamy treat. Different colors of quinoa are usually interchangeable, but for porridge like this I prefer to use white quinoa for its softer texture and neutral flavor. **Serves 4**

1½ cups white quinoa,
   rinsed well

1½ cups unsweetened
   coconut milk, or almond milk

1½ cups water

2 peaches, chopped

1 tablespoon honey

1 teaspoon vanilla extract

Pinch Celtic sea salt or
   kosher salt

1. In your pressure cooker, combine the quinoa, coconut milk, water, peaches, honey, vanilla, and salt. Lock the lid in place and set the cooker to High pressure for 1 minute.

2. When the cook time ends, let the pressure release naturally for 10 minutes; manually release any remaining pressure. Carefully remove the lid.

Substitution tip: Swap the peaches for your favorite stone fruit, or omit the peaches and top the cooked quinoa with fresh berries.

Per Serving: Calories: 298; Total Fat: 5g; Saturated Fat: 1g; Protein: 10g; Total Carbs: 53g; Fiber: 6g; Net Carbs: 47g; Cholesterol: 0mg

DAIRY-FREE, GLUTEN-FREE, VEGETARIAN

" . . . coconut milk with peaches and vanilla results in a sweet, creamy treat."

Chapter 3

MEATLESS MAINS

CURRIED CHICKPEA STEW

Prep time: 10 minutes / **Time to pressure:** 12 minutes / **Cook time:** 10 minutes / **Release time:** 5 minutes

This warm and cozy recipe was inspired by one of my favorite Indian take-out dishes, chana masala. Cream stirred in at the end mellows the curry powder's heat, so the final dish is only slightly spicy. It's delicious straight from the pot, but even better the next day once the flavors have had more time to meld. **Serves 6**

1 tablespoon unsalted butter

1 onion, chopped

1 tablespoon grated peeled fresh ginger

4 garlic cloves, minced

2 (15-ounce) cans chickpeas, drained

1 (14.5-ounce) can diced fire-roasted tomatoes

1 cup cauliflower florets

1 tablespoon garam masala

½ cup heavy (whipping) cream

1 teaspoon freshly squeezed lime juice

Celtic sea salt or kosher salt

1. On your pressure cooker, select Sauté. Put the butter in the cooker to melt.

2. Add the onion, ginger, and garlic. Cook for 3 minutes, or until softened.

3. Add the chickpeas, tomatoes, cauliflower, and garam masala. Lock the lid in place and set the cooker to High pressure for 6 minutes.

4. When the cook time ends, manually release the pressure.

5. Carefully remove the lid and stir in the heavy cream and lime juice. Season to taste with salt.

Substitution tip: For a vegan dish, use extra-virgin olive oil in place of the butter and substitute full-fat coconut milk for the heavy cream.

Per Serving: Calories: 303; Total Fat: 11g; Saturated Fat: 6g; Protein: 10g; Total Carbs: 43g; Fiber: 9g; Net Carbs: 34g; Cholesterol: 32mg

GLUTEN-FREE, NUT-FREE, VEGETARIAN

CHIMICHURRI PASTA

Prep time: 20 minutes / **Cook time:** 10 minutes

This one-pot pasta is inspired by my favorite pasta salad, and it's delicious served either hot or chilled. The ingredient list is simple, but don't let that fool you—chimichurri sauce is loaded with flavor. Boiling the pasta and asparagus together means you don't need to dirty a second pot. I like making this with whole-wheat pasta, but you can also use gluten-free pasta, if you prefer. **Serves 4**

Celtic sea salt or kosher salt

8 ounces whole-wheat pasta

1 pound asparagus, woody ends trimmed, cut into 1-inch pieces

½ cup Chimichurri Sauce (page 140)

2 cups fresh baby spinach, chopped

½ pint grape tomatoes, quartered

2 ounces crumbled feta cheese

Freshly ground black pepper

1. Bring a Dutch oven filled with salted water to a boil over high heat. Add the pasta and cook according to the package directions until al dente. Two minutes before the pasta is done, add the asparagus. When the pasta is al dente, drain and rinse with cold water.

2. Return the pasta and asparagus to the empty pot. Stir in the chimichurri sauce, baby spinach, tomatoes, and feta. Season to taste with salt and pepper.

Substitution tip: If you don't like asparagus or if it isn't in season, substitute fresh broccoli florets.

Per Serving: Calories: 402; Total Fat: 17g; Saturated Fat: 3g; Protein: 13g; Total Carbs: 48g; Fiber: 8g; Net Carbs: 40g; Cholesterol: 23mg

NUT-FREE, VEGETARIAN

LIGHTER FALAFEL

Prep time: 10 minutes / **Cook time:** 12 minutes per batch

Falafel is one of my favorite street foods. Using the air fryer to make it means you can have that classic fried texture without all the unhealthy oil. These are great stuffed into a pita with cucumber and tomato or on top of a salad with crumbled feta cheese and my All-Purpose Greek Dressing (page 137). **Serves 4**

2 (15-ounce) cans chickpeas, drained

1 onion, grated

4 garlic cloves, grated

¼ cup fresh parsley, chopped

1 teaspoon ground cumin

1 teaspoon extra-virgin olive oil

Olive oil cooking spray, for preparing the falafel

1. In a large resealable plastic bag, combine the chickpeas, onion, garlic, parsley, cumin, and olive oil. Seal the bag and massage the contents with your hands to mash the chickpeas and combine everything into a thick paste. Form the mixture into 16 tablespoon-size balls. Place them on your work surface and flatten slightly. Coat with olive oil cooking spray.

2. Working in batches as needed, place the patties into your air fryer's basket in a single layer. Fry at 370°F for 6 minutes per side.

Leftovers tip: Falafel also make a great high-protein snack. Serve them with hummus or Baba Ghanoush (page 121) for dipping.

Per Serving: Calories: 314; Total Fat: 4g; Saturated Fat: 1g; Protein: 13g; Total Carbs: 58g; Fiber: 11g; Net Carbs: 47g; Cholesterol: 0mg

DAIRY-FREE, GLUTEN-FREE, NUT-FREE, VEGAN, VEGETARIAN

ITALIAN EGGPLANT STACKS

Prep time: 15 minutes / **Cook time:** 20 minutes

When I was a kid, "eggplant cookies"—breaded and fried eggplant rounds—were one of my favorite foods. These eggplant stacks start with a baked version that is layered with roasted tomatoes, mozzarella cheese, and fresh basil for an elegant take on eggplant Parmesan. As the stacks are tall, they don't take up much space on your plate. I usually pair them with a simple salad to round things out. **Serves 4**

Extra-virgin olive oil, for preparing the sheet pan

1 large eggplant, cut into 12 rounds, about ¼ inch thick

1 large tomato, cut into 8 rounds, about ¼ inch thick

1 large egg, beaten

Freshly ground black pepper

½ cup seasoned Italian bread crumbs

1 (4-ounce) fresh mozzarella cheese log or ball, cut into 8 slices

8 fresh basil leaves

1. Preheat the oven to 450°F. Line a sheet pan with aluminum foil and drizzle the foil with olive oil.

2. Arrange the eggplant and tomato slices in a single layer on the prepared sheet pan. Brush the eggplant with the beaten egg and season with pepper. Sprinkle the eggplant with the bread crumbs. Bake for 20 minutes.

3. Top 4 eggplant slices, each with 1 slice of roasted tomato. Place 1 slice of mozzarella and 1 basil leaf on each tomato. Top each stack with another slice of eggplant, tomato, mozzarella, and 1 basil leaf. Top each stack with one last eggplant slice.

Substitution tip: Swap zucchini for the eggplant, if you prefer.

Per Serving: Calories: 154; Total Fat: 8g; Saturated Fat: 4g; Protein: 10g; Total Carbs: 13g; Fiber: 6g; Net Carbs: 7g; Cholesterol: 67mg

NUT-FREE, VEGETARIAN

PUMPKIN & LENTIL CHILI

Prep time: 5 minutes / **Cook time:** 10 hours

This protein-packed pumpkin and lentil chili is one of the first recipes I make every fall—I love the contrast of the subtly sweet pumpkin against the earthy beans and spicy chili powder. This chili is great on its own, but I also love serving it over a baked potato or with a side of corn bread. **Serves 6**

1 (15-ounce) can
  pumpkin purée

1 cup dried lentils

1 (15.5-ounce) can low-sodium
  black beans, drained

1 (14.5-ounce) can diced
  fire-roasted tomatoes

2½ cups Garden Vegetable
  Stock (page 135), or
  low-sodium store-bought
  vegetable stock

1 onion, chopped

1 green bell pepper, chopped

1 carrot, chopped

2 tablespoons gluten-free
  chili powder

Celtic sea salt or kosher salt

1. In your slow cooker, combine the pumpkin, lentils, black beans, tomatoes, vegetable stock, onion, green bell pepper, carrot, and chili powder.

2. Cover the cooker and set it to low heat. Cook for 10 hours, or until the lentils are soft. Season to taste with salt.

Ingredient tip: Be sure to use pure pumpkin purée, not pumpkin pie filling. You can also swap the pumpkin for puréed butternut squash.

Per Serving: Calories: 216; Total Fat: 2g; Saturated Fat: 1g; Protein: 13g; Total Carbs: 41g; Fiber: 17g; Net Carbs: 24g; Cholesterol: 0mg

DAIRY-FREE, GLUTEN-FREE, NUT-FREE, VEGAN, VEGETARIAN

MUSHROOM & FARRO "STROGANOFF"

Prep time: 5 minutes / **Cook time:** 30 minutes

Stroganoff is traditionally served over egg noodles, but this version is anything but traditional. I swap the noodles for nutty farro, add tons of mushrooms instead of beef, and serve the sour cream right on top instead of melted into the sauce. This recipe is one of my family's all-time favorites to help us warm up on cold winter nights.

Serves 4

1 tablespoon extra-virgin olive oil

1 onion, thinly sliced

8 ounces cremini mushrooms, sliced

1 tablespoon peppercorns

¾ cup dry sherry

2 cups Garden Vegetable Stock (page 135), or low-sodium store-bought vegetable stock

1 cup pearled farro

¼ cup sour cream

1. In a large skillet over medium heat, heat the olive oil.

2. When the oil is hot, add the onion. Cook for 5 minutes, or until softened.

3. Add the mushrooms and peppercorns. Cook for 5 minutes, or until deeply browned.

4. Add the sherry. Cook for 2 to 3 minutes, or until nearly dissolved.

5. Pour in the vegetable stock and bring the mixture to a boil.

6. Add the farro. Cook for 15 minutes until the farro is tender and the liquid is absorbed. Serve topped with the sour cream.

Substitution tip: We love the traditional taste of sour cream, but you can substitute fat-free plain Greek yogurt, if you prefer.

Per Serving: Calories: 182; Total Fat: 8g; Saturated Fat: 3g; Protein: 4g; Total Carbs: 17g; Fiber: 3g; Net Carbs: 14g; Cholesterol: 6mg

NUT-FREE, VEGETARIAN

CREAMY TOMATO SOUP WITH FARRO

Prep time: 10 minutes / **Cook time:** 8 hours

Creamy tomato soup is one of my favorite meals to eat on a wintery day. In this recipe, goat cheese gives more flavor than traditional heavy cream. Farro adds a slight nutty flavor and some texture to round out the meal. **Serves 4**

1 (28-ounce) can crushed fire-roasted tomatoes

½ cup pearled farro

4 garlic cloves, grated

1 onion, grated

1 carrot, grated

2 cups Garden Vegetable Stock (page 135), or low-sodium store-bought vegetable stock

2 ounces goat cheese

2 tablespoons fresh basil, thinly sliced

Celtic sea salt or kosher salt

1. In your slow cooker, combine the tomatoes, farro, garlic, onion, carrot, and vegetable stock.

2. Cover the cooker and set it to low heat. Cook for 8 hours.

3. Stir in the goat cheese and basil. Season to taste with salt.

Ingredient tip: Grating vegetables instead of dicing them helps them melt into the soup for a smoother texture—no blender required.

Per Serving: Calories: 166; Total Fat: 4g; Saturated Fat: 3g; Protein: 9g; Total Carbs: 27g; Fiber: 8g; Net Carbs: 19g; Cholesterol: 7mg

NUT-FREE, VEGETARIAN

TACO VEGGIE BURGERS & FRIES

Prep time: 10 minutes / **Cook time:** 40 to 45 minutes

Black beans and walnuts give these veggie burgers a meaty flavor and hearty texture. They're a great basic burger that you can season any way you want. My favorite way to make them is to season them with taco seasoning and top them with Cheddar cheese and creamy avocado. Depending on my mood, I'll either eat them on a bun or wrap them in crisp iceberg or green leaf lettuce. **Serves 4**

2 russet potatoes, halved lengthwise, each half cut into 6 wedges

2 tablespoons extra-virgin olive oil

Celtic sea salt or kosher salt

1 cup drained canned low-sodium black beans

1 carrot, grated

½ cup walnuts, finely chopped

¼ cup grated onion

1 (1.25-ounce) packet taco seasoning

4 slices Cheddar cheese (optional)

4 hamburger rolls, or lettuce leaves

1 avocado, sliced

1. Preheat the oven to 400°F.

2. Arrange the potato wedges in a single layer on one side of a sheet pan. Toss with the olive oil and generously season with salt.

3. In a medium bowl, using a heavy wooden spoon, mash the black beans. Stir in the carrot, walnuts, onion, and taco seasoning. Mix well to combine. Form the mixture into 4 patties and place them on the other side of the sheet pan.

4. Bake for 35 to 40 minutes, flipping the burgers halfway through the cooking time. Top each burger with 1 slice of cheese (if using) and return them to the oven for 2 to 3 minutes more to melt the cheese.

5. Serve the burgers on a roll or in lettuce leaves, topped with the avocado.

Leftovers tip: Leftover burgers reheat well in a lightly oiled skillet over medium heat for 2 to 3 minutes per side. Note: If making these ahead, do not add the cheese. Leftovers will keep, refrigerated in an airtight container, for 3 days.

Per Serving: Calories: 373; Total Fat: 23g; Saturated Fat: 3g; Protein: 10g; Total Carbs: 36g; Fiber: 11g; Net Carbs: 25g; Cholesterol: 3mg

VEGETARIAN

SWEET POTATO FRITTERS WITH CHIPOTLE SAUCE

Prep time: 10 minutes / **Cook time:** 15 minutes

This is a fun new-world twist on potato pancakes. The fritters themselves are sweet and a little salty, but the chipotle and yogurt dipping sauce really brings heat! If you're a fan of combining sweet and spicy flavors, you'll definitely love these. **Serves 4**

2 sweet potatoes, grated

3 cups fresh baby spinach, chopped

1 shallot, minced

2 large eggs, beaten

1 large egg white, beaten

½ cup all-purpose flour

2 or 3 tablespoons coconut oil, divided

Celtic sea salt

½ cup fat-free plain Greek yogurt

1 chipotle in adobo, minced

1 tablespoon freshly squeezed lime juice

1. Line a plate with paper towels and set aside.

2. In a large bowl, combine the grated sweet potatoes, spinach, shallot, eggs, egg white, and flour. Mix to combine.

3. In a large skillet over medium-high heat, melt 1 tablespoon of coconut oil.

4. Scoop in ½-cup portions of batter (I can usually fit 3 or 4 fritters without overcrowding the skillet). Fry for 2 minutes per side. Transfer to the plate and sprinkle with salt.

5. Add another tablespoon of coconut oil to the skillet and repeat step 4, continuing to add coconut oil before each batch, until all the batter is used.

6. In a small bowl, stir together the yogurt, chipotle, and lime juice.

7. Serve the sweet potato fritters with the chipotle dipping sauce.

Ingredient tip: Did you know chipotle peppers are really just smoked jalapeños? They're a great way to add smoky flavor to your recipes.

Per Serving (3 fritters with sauce): Calories: 242; Total Fat: 10g; Saturated Fat: 7g; Protein: 11g; Total Carbs: 29g; Fiber: 3g; Net Carbs: 26g; Cholesterol: 95mg

VEGETARIAN

TOFU WITH PEANUT SAUCE

Prep time: 5 minutes / **Cook time:** 8 minutes per batch

Tofu doesn't have much flavor on its own, but tossed in peanut sauce it's delicious! The air fryer makes quick work of this stir-fry. Dusting the tofu with cornstarch helps it come out extra crispy. I like to add a thinly sliced red bell pepper along with the broccoli for a pop of color and bright flavor. **Serves 4**

4 cups fresh broccoli florets

1 red bell pepper,
    thinly sliced

14 ounces extra-firm tofu,
    cut into 1-inch cubes

1 tablespoon cornstarch

¾ cup canned full-fat
    coconut milk

¼ cup smooth peanut butter

1 tablespoon grated peeled
    fresh ginger

1 tablespoon low-sodium
    soy sauce

1 tablespoon freshly
    squeezed lime juice

Celtic sea salt or kosher salt

4 tablespoons
    chopped peanuts

1. Depending on the size of your air fryer, you may need to work in batches. In your air fryer's basket, combine the broccoli and red bell pepper in a single layer.

2. In a large bowl, combine the tofu and cornstarch. Toss to coat. Arrange the tofu in a single layer on top of the broccoli and bell pepper. Fry at 390°F for 8 minutes.

3. While the stir-fry cooks, in a large bowl, whisk the coconut milk, peanut butter, ginger, soy sauce, and lime juice. Season to taste with salt.

4. Add the cooked vegetables and tofu to the peanut sauce and toss to coat.

5. Top each serving with 1 tablespoon of chopped peanuts.

Substitution tip: If you have a peanut allergy, this sauce is also great made with sunflower seed butter.

Per Serving: Calories: 393; Total Fat: 30g; Saturated Fat: 12g; Protein: 20g; Total Carbs: 21g; Fiber: 6g; Net Carbs: 14g; Cholesterol: 0mg

DAIRY-FREE, VEGAN, VEGETARIAN

FAJITA BURRITO BOWLS

Prep time: 5 minutes / **Time to pressure:** 10 minutes / **Cook time:** 15 minutes / **Pressure release:** 5 minutes

Burrito bowls have never been easier, thanks to electric pressure cookers. The rice, beans, onions, and pepper all cook together in just a few minutes. Add your favorite toppings—I like cheese, tomatoes, jalapeño, and cilantro. The rice and bean filling reheats really well, so this is a great recipe to meal prep for the week. Just add your toppings when you're ready to eat. **Serves 6**

1 cup uncooked long-grain brown rice

1 (16-ounce) can low-sodium pinto beans, undrained

1 cup Garden Vegetable Stock (page 135), or low-sodium store-bought vegetable stock

2 green bell peppers, sliced

2 red onions, sliced

1 teaspoon gluten-free chili powder

6 ounces shredded pepper Jack cheese

2 plum tomatoes, diced

1 jalapeño pepper, seeded and minced

¼ cup fresh cilantro, chopped

1. In your pressure cooker, combine the brown rice, pinto beans, vegetable stock, green bell peppers, red onions, and chili powder. Lock the lid in place and set the cooker to High pressure for 15 minutes.

2. When the cook time ends, let the pressure release naturally.

3. Scoop ½ cup of the rice filling into a dish. Top with cheese, tomato, jalapeño, and cilantro, as desired.

Substitution tip: Get creative with toppings—you can add anything from salsa or sour cream to shredded lettuce or sliced olives. You can also roll the filling into a flour tortilla for a more traditional burrito.

Per Serving: Calories: 264; Total Fat: 10g; Saturated Fat: 7g; Protein: 14g; Total Carbs: 31g; Fiber: 8g; Net Carbs: 23g; Cholesterol: 30mg

GLUTEN-FREE, NUT-FREE, VEGETARIAN

EGGPLANT & ASPARAGUS STIR-FRY

Prep time: 15 minutes / **Cook time:** 15 minutes

The honey and soy stir-fry sauce I use in this recipe is one of my favorites. It's easy to make and tastes great on everything from vegetables to pork. Here, I combine it with eggplant and asparagus in a nod to one of my beloved Chinese take-out dishes. It's a great recipe for when you feel like something on the lighter side. **Serves 6**

½ cup low-sodium soy sauce

⅓ cup clover honey

2 teaspoons cornstarch

2 teaspoons grated peeled fresh ginger

6 garlic cloves, minced

¼ teaspoon red pepper flakes (optional)

4 ounces dry rice noodles

2 tablespoons extra-virgin olive oil

2 pounds eggplant, peeled and diced

1 pound asparagus, woody ends trimmed, cut into 1-inch pieces

¼ cup cashews, chopped

1. In a small bowl, combine the soy sauce, honey, cornstarch, ginger, garlic, and red pepper flakes (if using). Stir well to mix. Set aside.

2. In a large deep skillet over high heat, bring 4 cups of water to a boil. Add the rice noodles. Cook for 2 minutes until tender. Drain and rinse with cold water. Set aside.

3. Return the skillet to high heat and heat the olive oil.

4. When the oil is hot, add the eggplant. Cook for 3 minutes.

5. Add the asparagus and ¼ cup of water. Cook for 2 minutes, stirring occasionally, or until the eggplant is tender and the water has evaporated.

6. Pour in the stir-fry sauce and cook for 1 minute to reduce.

7. Remove the skillet from the heat and stir in the rice noodles. Top with the cashews.

Ingredient tip: Be sure to use standard clover honey for this recipe. Fancier honey, such as wildflower or buckwheat, can have an overpowering flavor.

Per Serving: Calories: 270; Total Fat: 8g; Saturated Fat: 1g; Protein: 6g; Total Carbs: 50g; Fiber: 8g; Net Carbs: 42g; Cholesterol: 0mg

DAIRY-FREE, VEGETARIAN

SUMMER CORN & QUINOA CHOWDER

Prep time: 10 minutes / **Cook time:** 25 minutes

Corn chowder is one of my favorite ways to celebrate late-summer produce. This vegan version is full of new-world flavors such as quinoa and red bell pepper. I also add coconut milk because corn and cream is a match made in heaven. Basil stirred in at the end adds an extra pop of freshness. **Serves 4**

2 tablespoons extra-virgin olive oil

1 onion, chopped

2 celery stalks, thinly sliced

1 red bell pepper, chopped

Celtic sea salt or kosher salt

Freshly ground black pepper

2 Yukon Gold potatoes, diced

1 tablespoon all-purpose flour

4 cups Garden Vegetable Stock (page 135), or low-sodium store-bought vegetable stock

4 ears fresh corn, shucked, kernels cut from cob

½ cup quinoa, any color, rinsed well

½ cup canned full-fat coconut milk

2 tablespoons fresh basil, chopped

1. In a Dutch oven over medium-high heat, heat the olive oil.

2. Add the onion, celery, and red bell pepper. Season with salt and pepper. Cook for 5 minutes.

3. Add the potatoes. Cook for 3 minutes.

4. Stir in the flour.

5. Pour in the vegetable stock. Add the corn and quinoa. Bring to a boil and reduce to a simmer. Simmer for 15 minutes, or until the potatoes are soft.

6. Stir in the coconut milk and basil. Season to taste with salt and pepper.

Ingredient tip: Quinoa is a quick-cooking grain native to the Andes Mountains in South America. There are several varieties, from white to black and even purple! They all taste slightly different, but you can use any in this recipe.

Per Serving: Calories: 383; Total Fat: 19g; Saturated Fat: 10g; Protein: 9g; Total Carbs: 55g; Fiber: 8g; Net Carbs: 48g; Cholesterol: 0mg

DAIRY-FREE, VEGAN, VEGETARIAN

BUTTERNUT GOAT CHEESE FRITTATA

Prep time: 10 minutes / **Cook time:** 25 minutes

Most people think of frittatas as a breakfast food, but when you fill them with savory ingredients and serve them with a salad, they're also great for lunch or dinner. Sweet, roasted butternut squash and creamy goat cheese are a classic combination. Crispy Swiss chard rounds out this air-fried frittata's fall harvest vibe. *Serves 4*

1 medium butternut squash, diced (about 2 cups)

2 cups sliced Swiss chard

2 tablespoons extra-virgin olive oil

Celtic sea salt or kosher salt

Freshly ground black pepper

8 large eggs

2 ounces soft goat cheese, divided

¼ teaspoon red pepper flakes

1. In a 6-inch round cake pan, combine the squash, Swiss chard, and olive oil. Season with salt and pepper. Place the pan in your air fryer's basket. Fry at 370°F for 10 minutes.

2. Transfer half the vegetables to another 6-inch round cake pan. Set aside.

3. Crack 4 eggs into the first cake pan and whisk well. Crumble in half the goat cheese and sprinkle with a pinch of red pepper flakes. Air fry at 370°F for 6 minutes, or until the frittata's center is puffed and lightly brown.

4. Repeat with the remaining ingredients to make a second frittata.

Substitution tip: This recipe is really versatile—swap sweet potato for the butternut squash or kale for the Swiss chard.

Per Serving: Calories: 276; Total Fat: 20g; Saturated Fat: 6g; Protein: 16g; Total Carbs: 10g; Fiber: 2g; Net Carbs: 8g; Cholesterol: 378mg

GLUTEN-FREE, NUT-FREE, VEGETARIAN

Chapter 4

CHICKEN

ROASTED CHICKEN WITH CARROTS & CHICKPEAS

Prep time: 5 minutes / **Cook time:** 1 hour

Roasted chicken is one of my favorite foods, but I rarely have time to make it. These crispy chicken thighs are the next best thing. Using a Dutch oven lets you crisp the chicken skin on the stovetop before finishing the thighs in the oven. Parsley, rosemary, and shallot give them a rustic Italian flavor that makes this dish perfect for a cold, rainy night. A delicious chickpea and carrot stew completes this hearty one-pot meal. *Serves 4*

1 tablespoon extra-virgin olive oil

4 bone-in, skin-on chicken thighs

Celtic sea salt or kosher salt

Freshly ground black pepper

6 carrots, sliced

1 teaspoon honey

2 cups drained canned chickpeas, or 1½ cups cooked chickpeas

½ shallot, finely chopped

2 tablespoons fresh parsley, chopped

¼ teaspoon dried rosemary, crushed

1. Preheat the oven to 375°F.

2. In a Dutch oven over medium heat, heat the olive oil.

3. Season the chicken with salt and pepper. Carefully place the chicken, skin-side down, in the hot oil. Cook for 8 to 10 minutes, or until golden brown and crisp. Turn the chicken skin-side up.

4. Add the carrots, honey, and chickpeas. Transfer the pot to the oven and roast, uncovered, for 40 to 45 minutes until cooked through.

5. Remove the chicken from the pot. Stir in the shallot, parsley, and rosemary. Season to taste with salt and pepper. Serve the chicken with the stew on the side.

Ingredient tip: Shallots are mild onions with a subtle flavor similar to garlic or leeks. Because they're so mild, they don't need to be cooked in this recipe. If you prefer, substitute 1 tablespoon of finely chopped red onion and add it in step 4.

Per Serving: Calories: 453; Total Fat: 24g; Saturated Fat: 8g; Protein: 24g; Total Carbs: 38g; Fiber: 9g; Net Carbs: 29g; Cholesterol: 98mg

DAIRY-FREE, GLUTEN-FREE, NUT-FREE

SHEET PAN CHICKEN TERIYAKI

Prep time: 10 minutes / **Cook time:** 15 minutes

Prepared teriyaki sauce is loaded with sugar, but it's easy to make your own low-sugar version with pantry basics. I love using it on this sheet pan chicken teriyaki, which is basically a giant stir-fry made in the oven. I add fresh pineapple to play up the teriyaki's sweetness and top it off with cashews for a little crunch. **Serves 4**

¼ cup low-sodium soy sauce

2 tablespoons mirin

1 tablespoon honey

1 pound boneless, skinless chicken breast, thinly sliced

1 cup fresh pineapple chunks

2 cups broccoli florets

1 red bell pepper, thinly sliced

1 cup sugar snap peas, strings removed

¼ cup cashews, roughly chopped

1. Preheat the oven to 400°F.

2. In a large bowl, whisk the soy sauce, mirin, and honey.

3. Add the chicken and stir to coat.

4. Add the pineapple, broccoli, red bell pepper, and peas. Stir to coat. Pour the contents onto a sheet pan. Bake for 15 minutes, or until the chicken is cooked through.

5. Stir in the cashews.

Ingredient tip: Mirin is a sweet Japanese cooking wine similar to sake that gives teriyaki its hallmark flavor. Once you buy it, it will keep, refrigerated, for a very long time.

Per Serving: Calories: 262; Total Fat: 7g; Saturated Fat: 1g; Protein: 28g; Total Carbs: 24g; Fiber: 3g; Net Carbs: 21g; Cholesterol: 72mg

DAIRY-FREE

AIR FRYER CHICKEN PARMESAN WITH BABY BROCCOLINI

Prep time: 15 minutes / **Cook time:** 20 minutes

Chicken Parmesan is a classic comfort food, but one usually loaded with fat from being deep-fried and smothered with cheese. For this lighter take, I use an air fryer and swap the mozzarella cheese for provolone, which has a mildly smoky flavor. The chicken bakes on a bed of garlicky broccolini, which makes the perfect side dish. For a more substantial meal, add both the chicken and broccolini to a whole-grain roll for an awesome chicken Parm sandwich. **Serves 4**

---

1 bunch broccolini (about 4 stems), or 1 cup broccoli florets

1 garlic clove, slivered

Olive oil cooking spray, for preparing the vegetables

2 large eggs, beaten

½ cup seasoned Italian bread crumbs

2 boneless, skinless chicken breasts

¼ cup all-purpose flour

Celtic sea salt or kosher salt

Freshly ground black pepper

½ cup Super Simple Marinara (page 132)

4 ounces provolone cheese, sliced

1. In your air fryer's basket, combine the broccolini and garlic. Spritz the vegetables with cooking spray.

2. Place the beaten eggs in a shallow bowl and the bread crumbs in a second shallow bowl. Set aside.

3. Cut the chicken breasts in half. Split each half crosswise, without cutting all the way through, to form 4 thin cutlets. Sprinkle the chicken with flour and season with salt and pepper.

4. Dredge each cutlet in egg, remove, and coat with bread crumbs. Place the breaded chicken into the air fryer, on top of the broccolini. Depending on the size of your fryer basket, you may need to fry in two batches. Fry at 370°F for 15 minutes.

5. Top the chicken with marinara and cheese and fry at 370°F for 5 minutes more until the cheese melts and the chicken is cooked through.

Substitution tip: For a gluten-free option, swap the flour and bread crumbs for almond flour and crushed gluten-free cornflakes.

Per Serving: Calories: 259; Total Fat: 12g; Saturated Fat: 6g; Protein: 26g; Total Carbs: 13g; Fiber: 2g; Net Carbs: 11g; Cholesterol: 145mg

NUT-FREE

LEMON CHICKEN TORTELLINI SOUP

Prep time: 10 minutes / **Cook time:** 10 minutes

This is one of my favorite springtime soups—it's a perfect feel-good soup when you have a cold. The garlic, leeks, and Parmesan give the broth a slightly floral flavor that reminds me a little of wonton soup, but the lemon juice makes it bright and vibrant. Because this soup is so simple, the quality of the individual ingredients really matters. I highly recommend using homemade chicken stock for the best flavor. **Serves 4**

1 tablespoon extra-virgin olive oil

1 garlic clove, minced

1 leek, white and green parts, thinly sliced

2 carrots, sliced

6 cups Chicken Stock (page 133), or low-sodium store-bought chicken stock

½ ounce grated Parmesan cheese

9 ounces fresh cheese tortellini

½ cup peas, fresh or frozen

2 cups fresh baby spinach

Juice of 1 lemon

Celtic sea salt or kosher salt

Freshly ground black pepper

1. In a Dutch oven over medium-high heat, heat the olive oil.

2. Add the garlic, leek, and carrots. Cook for 5 minutes, or until softened.

3. Add the chicken stock and Parmesan. Bring to a boil.

4. Stir in the tortellini. Boil for 5 minutes, or until the tortellini are cooked through.

5. Stir in the peas, spinach, and lemon juice. Season to taste with salt and pepper.

Ingredient tip: Zest the lemon before you juice it and freeze the zest for the next time you want to add lemony zip to a recipe.

Per Serving: Calories: 308; Total Fat: 8g; Saturated Fat: 1g; Protein: 16g; Total Carbs: 43g; Fiber: 2g; Net Carbs: 41g; Cholesterol: 15mg

NUT-FREE

SHEET PAN BARBECUE CHICKEN DINNER

Prep time: 15 minutes / **Cook time:** 35 minutes

Barbecue chicken is a summertime classic, but now you can enjoy it year-round thanks to this easy sheet pan recipe. Instead of a vegetable, like corn or green beans, I like serving this chicken with spicy mango salad to keep the summertime theme going. If you have extra barbecue sauce, use it on your crispy potato wedges. **Serves 4**

FOR THE CHICKEN AND POTATOES

4 red potatoes, cut into wedges

1 tablespoon extra-virgin olive oil

Celtic sea salt

Freshly ground black pepper

4 boneless, skinless chicken thighs

¼ cup Maple Barbecue Sauce (page 136)

FOR THE MANGO SALAD

1 mango, peeled and diced

1 jalapeño pepper, seeded and minced

½ red onion, minced

¼ cup fresh cilantro, chopped

Juice of 1 lime

Celtic sea salt

TO MAKE THE CHICKEN AND POTATOES

1. Preheat the oven to 400°F.

2. Arrange the potato wedges in a single layer on one side of a sheet pan. Drizzle with olive oil and season with salt and pepper.

3. Place the chicken thighs on the other side of the sheet pan. Brush the chicken with barbecue sauce. Bake for 25 to 35 minutes until the chicken is cooked through and the potatoes are soft.

TO MAKE THE MANGO SALAD

While the chicken cooks, in a medium bowl, stir together the mango, jalapeño, red onion, cilantro, lime juice, and a pinch of salt. Mix well. Let stand at room temperature for 5 minutes.

Repurpose tip: Make a double batch of mango salad—it's also great on tortilla chips or as an addition to Fajita Burrito Bowls (page 43).

Per Serving: Calories: 412; Total Fat: 10g; Saturated Fat: 2g; Protein: 27g; Total Carbs: 56g; Fiber: 6g; Net Carbs: 50g; Cholesterol: 95mg

DAIRY-FREE, GLUTEN-FREE, NUT-FREE

CHICKEN ENCHILADA SWEET POTATO NOODLES

- -

Prep time: 15 minutes / **Cook time:** 20 minutes

- -

I love the balance of sweet and spicy flavors in this easy skillet dinner. Everything from the potatoes to the beans to the cilantro plays a role in hitting all the right notes. Be sure not to skip the cheese and lime sprinkled over the top. Together, they add a pop of saltiness and acidity that really make this dish sing. **Serves 4**

- -

1 pound boneless, skinless chicken breast, diced

2 tablespoons all-purpose flour

Celtic sea salt or kosher salt

Freshly ground black pepper

2 tablespoons extra-virgin olive oil

1 large sweet potato, spiralized

1 (15.5-ounce) can low-sodium black beans, drained

½ onion, diced

1 cup Homemade Enchilada Sauce (page 139)

2 cups fresh baby spinach

¼ cup fresh cilantro, chopped

¼ cup feta or Cotija cheese crumbles

1 lime, quartered

1. In a large bowl, toss the chicken with the flour to coat. Season with salt and pepper.

2. In a large skillet over medium-high heat, heat the olive oil.

3. Add the chicken. Cook for 3 to 4 minutes, stirring once or twice, or until lightly browned.

4. Add the sweet potato, black beans, onion, and enchilada sauce. Stir to combine. Cover the skillet and simmer for 10 minutes.

5. Stir in the spinach and cilantro, stirring until wilted.

6. Top the dish with the cheese and serve with the lime wedges for squeezing.

- -

Substitution tip: I like to use spiralized sweet potatoes in this recipe—their shape is just so fun! If you don't have a spiralizer, many grocery stores sell spiralized vegetables in the refrigerated section of the produce department. Alternatively, cut the sweet potato into ¼-inch dice.

Per Serving: Calories: 337; Total Fat: 12g; Saturated Fat: 2g; Protein: 31g; Total Carbs: 25g; Fiber: 7g; Net Carbs: 18g; Cholesterol: 80mg

- -

NUT-FREE

WHITE PIZZA WITH CHICKEN & RED PEPPERS

Prep time: 5 minutes / **Cook time:** 10 to 12 minutes for each pizza

The intense, hot cooking temperatures of air fryers mean they work perfectly as a pizza oven. The crust cooks up perfectly crisp and the cheese gets so melty—I actually prefer it to baking pizza in my conventional oven. This version, topped with chicken, red pepper, and zucchini, is one of my favorites. The ingredients are simple, but together they have a ton of flavor. Plus it's faster than delivery! *Serves 4*

13 ounces pizza dough, at room temperature

2 tablespoons extra-virgin olive oil

4 garlic cloves, minced

1½ cups shredded part-skim mozzarella cheese

1 boneless, skinless chicken breast, thinly sliced

1 red bell pepper, thinly sliced

1 small zucchini, diced

1. Divide the pizza dough in half and flatten each half into an 8-inch round. Coat each round lightly with olive oil and sprinkle each with half of the minced garlic. Top each with ¾ cup of cheese and half each of the chicken, red bell pepper, and zucchini.

2. Place one round in your air fryer's basket. Fry at 375° F for 10 to 12 minutes, or until the dough is cooked through.

3. Remove the pizza from the air fryer and cut it into 4 pieces. Repeat with the second pizza.

Ingredient tip: Don't worry about precooking the chicken. It will cook along with the pizza and it stays super juicy!

Per Serving: Calories: 232; Total Fat: 12g; Saturated Fat: 2g; Protein: 13g; Total Carbs: 22g; Fiber: 2g; Net Carbs: 20g; Cholesterol: 26mg

NUT-FREE

CHICKEN & QUINOA SKILLET

Prep time: 15 minutes / **Cook time:** 35 minutes

This cheesy chicken and quinoa skillet is pure Tex-Mex comfort food. The recipe itself is pretty basic, but you can jazz it up with hot sauce or your favorite taco toppings such as fat-free sour cream, fresh cilantro, or sliced avocado. **Serves 6**

1 tablespoon extra-virgin olive oil

1 pound boneless, skinless chicken breast, cut into 1-inch pieces

1 small yellow onion, diced

2 garlic cloves, minced

1 jalapeño pepper, seeded and minced

1 (15.5-ounce) can low-sodium black beans, drained

12 ounces no-salt-added chopped tomatoes in purée

1 cup water

1 tablespoon dried oregano

1 cup quinoa, any color (I usually use tricolor), rinsed well

6 ounces sharp Cheddar cheese, shredded

4 scallions, white and green parts, sliced

1. In a large deep-sided skillet over medium-high heat, heat the olive oil.

2. Add the chicken. Cook for 7 to 8 minutes, stirring occasionally, or until browned.

3. Add the onion, garlic, and jalapeño. Cook for 4 to 5 minutes, or until just softened.

4. Pour in the black beans, tomatoes, and water. Add the oregano. Bring the mixture to a boil.

5. Stir in the quinoa. Cook for 15 minutes, or until the quinoa is cooked and most of the liquid has evaporated.

6. Spread an even layer of cheese over the top of the dish. Cover the skillet and cook for 3 to 4 minutes to melt the cheese. Top with the sliced scallions before serving.

Leftovers tip: Wrap leftovers in lettuce leaves for a fresh take on a burrito.

Per Serving: Calories: 422; Total Fat: 16g; Saturated Fat: 7g; Protein: 33g; Total Carbs: 37g; Fiber: 9g; Net Carbs: 28g; Cholesterol: 78mg

GLUTEN-FREE, NUT-FREE

THAI BASIL CHICKEN

Prep time: 10 minutes / **Cook time:** 15 minutes

I'm terrible at gardening, but one thing I can always seem to grow without problems is basil. Every August, my plant gets huge! When I get tired of pesto, I make Thai basil chicken, inspired by one of my favorite take-out meals. To keep things on the lighter side and help it cook faster, I serve it with cauliflower rice instead of white rice.

Serves 4

1 tablespoon extra-virgin olive oil

2 boneless, skinless chicken breasts, thinly sliced

1 Thai chile pepper, seeded and minced

2 red bell peppers, thinly sliced

2 onions, thinly sliced

3 tablespoons fish sauce

2 tablespoons low-sodium soy sauce

1 teaspoon rice vinegar

4 cups cauliflower rice

¼ cup fresh basil leaves

1 lime, quartered

1. In a large skillet over high heat, heat the olive oil.

2. Add the chicken. Cook for 3 to 4 minutes, stirring once or twice, or until lightly browned.

3. Add the chile pepper, red bell peppers, onions, fish sauce, soy sauce, and vinegar. Cook for 5 minutes until the vegetables are soft.

4. Add the cauliflower rice. Cook for 3 minutes until softened.

5. Stir in the basil. Serve with the lime wedges for squeezing.

Substitution tip: If you're not in the mood for chicken, this recipe is also great made with pork or shrimp.

Per Serving: Calories: 164; Total Fat: 5g; Saturated Fat: 1g; Protein: 17g; Total Carbs: 16g; Fiber: 5g; Net Carbs: 11g; Cholesterol: 33mg

DAIRY-FREE, NUT-FREE

SHEET PAN JERK CHICKEN WITH POTATOES & GREEN BEANS

Prep time: 10 minutes / **Cook time:** 40 minutes

If it's summer, you'll find me making crispy jerk chicken thighs and potatoes on the grill. I adapted that recipe for a sheet pan recipe so we can enjoy it year-round. Adding carrots and green beans turns it into a complete meal. *Serves 4*

4 bone-in chicken thighs, skin removed and discarded

1 tablespoon jerk seasoning

1 pound baby Yukon Gold potatoes

4 carrots, sliced

1 pound green beans, trimmed

1 tablespoon extra-virgin olive oil

Celtic sea salt or kosher salt

Freshly ground black pepper

1. Preheat the oven to 450°F.

2. Line a sheet pan with parchment paper. Place the chicken thighs on one side of the sheet pan. Rub each thigh with a light coating of jerk seasoning.

3. On the other side of the pan, combine the potatoes, carrots, and green beans. Drizzle with olive oil and season with salt and pepper.

4. Roast for 35 to 40 minutes, or until the potatoes are tender and the chicken is cooked through.

Ingredient tip: Jerk seasoning is a flavorful Caribbean blend containing allspice, Scotch bonnet pepper, and other warm spices. There are two types of jerk—a wet marinade that comes in a jar and a dry rub, which tends not to be quite as spicy. For this recipe, use the dry seasoning and remember, a little goes a long way.

Per Serving: Calories: 327; Total Fat: 11g; Saturated Fat: 1g; Protein: 24g; Total Carbs: 38g; Fiber: 9g; Net Carbs: 29g; Cholesterol: 34mg

DAIRY-FREE, GLUTEN-FREE, NUT-FREE

CHICKEN CHORIZO & POTATOES

Prep time: 10 minutes / **Cook time:** 30 minutes

This easy sheet pan dinner features tender potatoes, smoky chorizo, and roasted broccoli seasoned with paprika, oregano, and parsley. It's one of my go-to weeknight dinners because it's so good! **Serves 4**

1 pound small red potatoes, halved

1 head broccoli, cut into florets (about 4 cups)

2 tablespoons extra-virgin olive oil

2 teaspoons paprika

1 pound chicken chorizo, cut into rounds

3 tablespoons chopped green olives

1 tablespoon chopped fresh parsley

1 tablespoon chopped fresh oregano leaves

1. Preheat the oven to 400°F.

2. In a large bowl, combine the potatoes, broccoli, olive oil, and paprika. Mix well. Pour the vegetables onto a sheet pan. Scatter the chorizo over the potatoes.

3. Bake for 20 to 30 minutes, stirring halfway through the baking time, until the potatoes are tender.

4. Remove from the oven and stir in the olives, parsley, and oregano.

Ingredient tip: Chorizo is a slightly spicy sausage flavored with smoked paprika. Chicken chorizo can be found in most major supermarkets but, if you can't find it, substitute smoked pork chorizo.

Per Serving: Calories: 366; Total Fat: 19g; Saturated Fat: 4g; Protein: 26g; Total Carbs: 28g; Fiber: 7g; Net Carbs: 21g; Cholesterol: 70mg

DAIRY-FREE, GLUTEN-FREE, NUT-FREE

RED CURRY RAMEN

Prep time: 5 minutes / **Time to pressure:** 17 minutes / **Cook time:** 25 minutes / **Release time:** 5 minutes

This recipe was inspired by a special they had at our local ramen shop a few years ago. It was an instant classic from the first time I tasted it, and I crave it all the time. Red curry paste, shiitake mushrooms, and sesame oil add depth and flavor to the broth. It's delicious at its most basic, but sliced scallions and boiled egg really take it over the top. **Serves 4**

6 cups Chicken Stock (page 133), or low-sodium store-bought chicken stock

1 tablespoon grated peeled fresh ginger

1 tablespoon red curry paste

1 pound boneless, skinless chicken breast

3½ ounces shiitake mushrooms, sliced

¼ cup rice vinegar

2 tablespoons sesame oil

9 ounces ramen noodles, preferably organic

2 scallions, white and green parts, sliced (optional)

2 Pressure-Cooked Hard-boiled Eggs (page 138), halved (optional)

1. In your pressure cooker, combine the chicken stock, ginger, curry paste, chicken, mushrooms, vinegar, and sesame oil. Lock the lid in place and set the cooker to High pressure for 20 minutes.

2. When the cook time ends, manually release the pressure.

3. Carefully remove the lid and remove the chicken from the pot.

4. Add the ramen noodles. Let sit, uncovered, for 5 minutes, or until soft.

5. Shred the chicken and return it to the pot. Stir to combine.

6. Top the soup with the scallions and eggs (if using).

Ingredient tip: Ramen has come a long way since college. Skip the 25-cent packets and look for organic noodles made with minimal ingredients. If they come with a seasoning packet, throw it away—you don't need it.

Per Serving: Calories: 334; Total Fat: 15g; Saturated Fat: 3g; Protein: 35g; Total Carbs: 10g; Fiber: 1g; Net Carbs: 9g; Cholesterol: 154mg

DAIRY-FREE, NUT-FREE

CRISPY CHICKEN & WATERMELON SALAD

Prep time: 10 minutes / **Cook time:** 20 minutes

The first time I tasted a salad with watermelon, feta, and walnuts, I was hooked. The sweet watermelon and salty cheese go so well together, and nuts give it the perfect amount of crunch. I add crispy air-fried chicken to this recipe to up the protein and transform it into a complete meal. Any lettuce can work, but I love arugula for its peppery flavor and ability to withstand the melon's high moisture level. **Serves 4**

2 large eggs, beaten

½ cup plain bread crumbs

1 pound chicken
    breast cutlets

¼ cup all-purpose flour

Celtic sea salt or kosher salt

Freshly ground black pepper

Olive oil cooking spray, for
    coating the chicken

6 cups arugula

2 cups cubed watermelon

4 ounces crumbled
    feta cheese

¼ red onion, thinly sliced

2 tablespoons
    chopped walnuts

¼ cup balsamic vinegar

2 tablespoons extra-virgin
    olive oil

1. Place the beaten eggs in a shallow bowl and the bread crumbs in a second shallow bowl.

2. Sprinkle the chicken with the flour and season with salt and pepper. Dredge the chicken in the egg, remove, and coat with the bread crumbs. Spritz the coated chicken with cooking spray. Place the breaded chicken into your air fryer's basket. Fry at 370°F for 20 minutes, turning halfway through the cooking time. Cut into bite-size pieces.

3. In a large salad bowl, combine the cooked chicken with the arugula, watermelon, cheese, red onion, walnuts, vinegar, and olive oil. Toss to combine. Generously season with salt and pepper.

Substitution tip: If you prefer, use ¼ cup of my All-Purpose Greek Dressing (page 137) instead of oil and vinegar.

Per Serving: Calories: 415; Total Fat: 19g; Saturated Fat: 6g; Protein: 37g; Total Carbs: 25g; Fiber: 2g; Net Carbs: 23g; Cholesterol: 183mg

BALSAMIC CHICKEN & MUSHROOMS

Prep time: 10 minutes / **Cook time:** 15 minutes

Balsamic chicken is one of the most popular recipes on my site, so it's only fitting that I include a version in this book. To turn it into a complete one-pot meal, I add zucchini noodles and cherry tomatoes—both excellent choices, as is the decision to use quick-cooking chicken cutlets. **Serves 4**

1 pound chicken
   breast cutlets

2 teaspoons all-purpose flour

Celtic sea salt or kosher salt

Freshly ground black pepper

1 tablespoon extra-virgin
   olive oil

6 ounces cremini
   mushrooms, sliced

¼ cup Chicken Stock
   (page 133), or low-sodium
   store-bought chicken stock

2 tablespoons
   balsamic vinegar

10 ounces zucchini noodles

½ cup cherry
   tomatoes, halved

2 tablespoons fresh
   parsley, chopped

1. Sprinkle the chicken with the flour and season with salt and pepper.

2. In a large skillet over medium-high heat, heat the olive oil.

3. Add the chicken. Cook for 2 minutes per side to brown. Remove the chicken from the skillet and turn the heat to low.

4. Add the mushrooms to the skillet. Cook for 5 minutes, stirring occasionally, until deeply browned.

5. Add the chicken stock and vinegar. Bring the mixture to a simmer.

6. Add the zucchini noodles and tomatoes. Return the chicken to the pan. Return to a simmer and cook for 5 minutes, or until the chicken is cooked through.

7. Sprinkle with the parsley and season to taste with salt and pepper.

Substitution tip: For a different take on this recipe, omit the zucchini noodles and serve the chicken over mashed potatoes.

Per Serving: Calories: 187; Total Fat: 5g; Saturated Fat: 1g; Protein: 29g; Total Carbs: 7g; Fiber: 2g; Net Carbs: 5g; Cholesterol: 65mg

DAIRY-FREE, NUT-FREE

KOREAN PULLED CHICKEN LETTUCE CUPS

Prep time: 10 minutes / **Cook time:** 6 hours

This Korean-inspired chicken recipe is a lighter, fresher take on Korean tacos. The shredded chicken has a little bit of a kick to it, but the fresh lettuce and pickled vegetables tone it down. For a heartier meal, swap the lettuce wraps for flour tortillas.

Serves 4

1 pound boneless, skinless
  chicken breasts

⅓ cup chili-garlic sauce

¼ cup low-sodium soy sauce

3 tablespoons honey

3 tablespoons rice
  wine vinegar

Butter lettuce leaves,
  for serving

Quick cucumber pickles (see
  page 122), for serving

Shredded carrots, for serving

Sliced scallions, white and
  green parts, for serving

1. In your slow cooker, combine the chicken, chili-garlic sauce, soy sauce, honey, and vinegar. Cover the cooker and set it to low heat. Cook for 6 hours.

2. Shred the chicken and return it to the pot. Let stand for 5 minutes to soak up the sauce.

3. Serve the chicken in lettuce cups, topped with pickles, carrots, and scallions.

Make-ahead tip: Combine your slow cooker ingredients in a large resealable plastic bag the night before. All you have to do in the morning is pour the contents into your slow cooker and turn it on.

Per Serving: Calories: 266; Total Fat: 2g; Saturated Fat: 0g; Protein: 28g; Total Carbs: 33g; Fiber: 2g; Net Carbs: 31g; Cholesterol: 65g

DAIRY-FREE, NUT-FREE

OVEN-ROASTED TANDOORI CHICKEN THIGHS

Prep time: 10 minutes / **Cook time:** 40 minutes

There's a great Indian restaurant around the corner from my house, so it's hard to resist the temptation to grab take-out. Luckily, this Indian-spiced chicken recipe is easy enough that I have no excuse when a craving kicks in. It's inspired by tandoori, which is traditionally cooked in a super-hot clay oven. To mimic the char that traditional tandoori has, place your sheet pan under the broiler for 5 minutes after the chicken is cooked through. Either way, this meal is packed with flavor. Serves 4

½ cup fat-free plain Greek yogurt

1 tablespoon grated peeled fresh ginger

1 teaspoon garam masala

½ teaspoon ground turmeric

1 tablespoon freshly squeezed lemon juice

Celtic sea salt or kosher salt

4 boneless, skinless chicken thighs

1 acorn squash, cut into 8 wedges

1 small head cauliflower, cut into florets (about 2 cups)

4 carrots, sliced

1 large tomato, cut into 8 thick wedges

1 tablespoon extra-virgin olive oil

Freshly ground black pepper

1. Preheat the oven to 450°F.

2. In a large bowl, stir together the yogurt, ginger, garam masala, turmeric, lemon juice, and a pinch of salt. Add the chicken thighs and turn to coat.

3. Place the acorn squash, cauliflower, carrots, and tomato on a sheet pan. Drizzle with the olive oil. Season with salt and pepper. Spread the vegetables into a single layer. Nestle the chicken into the vegetables.

4. Bake for 25 to 35 minutes, or until the chicken is cooked through. If desired, broil the chicken for 5 minutes more to crisp it.

Leftovers tip: If you have leftover chicken, it makes great chicken salad! Dice it and combine with chopped celery and onion, fat-free plain Greek yogurt, lemon juice, and fresh cilantro.

Per Serving: Calories: 273; Total Fat: 8g; Saturated Fat: 2g; Protein: 28g; Total Carbs: 24g; Fiber: 5g; Net Carbs: 19g; Cholesterol: 96mg

GLUTEN-FREE, NUT-FREE

LEMON CHICKEN & RICE WITH ARTICHOKES & OLIVES

Prep time: 5 minutes / **Cook time:** 25 minutes

Artichoke hearts, lemon juice, and Kalamata olives give this simple chicken and rice dish a Greek vibe that I love. Cooking the rice in chicken stock instead of water adds even more flavor. I make this dish in my Dutch oven, but a saucepan with a tightly fitting lid works just as well. This recipe is also great made with brown rice—just add 10 minutes to the cooking time. *Serves 4*

---

2 tablespoons extra-virgin olive oil

1 pound boneless, skinless chicken breasts, diced

Celtic sea salt or kosher salt

Freshly ground black pepper

2½ cups Chicken Stock (page 133), or low-sodium store-bought chicken stock

1 onion, diced

1 cup uncooked long-grain white rice

1 can artichoke heart quarters, drained

4 cups fresh spinach

Juice of 1 lemon

½ cup whole pitted Kalamata olives

1. In a Dutch oven over medium-high heat, heat the olive oil.

2. When the oil is hot, add the chicken. Season with salt and pepper. Cook for 3 to 4 minutes, stirring occasionally, to brown.

3. Add the chicken stock, onion, rice, artichokes, spinach, lemon juice, and olives. Cover the pot and cook for 20 minutes, or until the liquid is absorbed and the rice is cooked through.

Ingredient tip: Look for artichoke hearts packed in water, not oil. If you prefer, frozen artichokes also work well. Throw them into the pot straight from the freezer—no need to thaw first.

Per Serving: Calories: 418; Total Fat: 11g; Saturated Fat: 1g; Protein: 34g; Total Carbs: 47g; Fiber: 6g; Net Carbs: 41g; Cholesterol: 65g

---

DAIRY-FREE, GLUTEN-FREE, NUT-FREE

HONEY MUSTARD CHICKEN THIGHS

Prep time: 5 minutes / **Cook time:** 8 hours

This recipe is super simple but surprisingly tasty. The creamy honey mustard sauce is loosely inspired by Carolina barbecue sauce and has a bit of tang from the vinegar. You can keep the chicken thighs whole, but I love shredding them and returning them to the pot so they can soak up every last bit of sauce. You might expect green beans to get mushy after being cooked for so long, but they actually come out perfectly. **Serves 4**

1½ pounds boneless, skinless chicken thighs

1½ pounds baby potatoes

4 ounces green beans

¼ cup Dijon mustard

¼ cup honey

2 tablespoons apple cider vinegar

In your slow cooker, combine the chicken, potatoes, green beans, mustard, honey, and vinegar. Cover the cooker and set it to high heat. Cook for 8 hours.

Ingredient tip: Be sure to use creamy Dijon-style mustard in this recipe. Whole-grain versions won't make the same kind of creamy sauce.

Per Serving: Calories: 398; Total Fat: 8g; Saturated Fat: 2g; Protein: 37g; Total Carbs: 47g; Fiber: 7g; Net Carbs: 40g; Cholesterol: 143mg

DAIRY-FREE, GLUTEN-FREE, NUT-FREE

Chapter 5

MEAT

GOULASH SOUP

Growing up, Hungarian goulash made a regular appearance on our dinner table. It had totally fallen off my radar until a few years ago when I stumbled on an Eastern European restaurant not far from us. Their goulash soup was warm, brothy, and the kind of meal I crave every time it snows. Thanks to the pressure cooker, it can be on the table in a little over an hour. *Serves 4*

2 tablespoons extra-virgin olive oil

1 pound boneless chuck roast, cut into ½-inch pieces

Celtic sea salt or kosher salt

Freshly ground black pepper

4 garlic cloves, minced

4 cups Chicken Stock (page 133), or low-sodium store-bought chicken stock

2 carrots, sliced

2 celery stalks, thinly sliced

1 onion, diced

1 red bell pepper, chopped

¼ cup sweet Hungarian paprika

1 bay leaf

2 tablespoons red wine vinegar

1. On your pressure cooker, select Sauté. Pour in the olive oil to heat.

2. Add the beef. Cook for 3 to 4 minutes, stirring once or twice, until browned. Season with salt and pepper.

3. Stir in the garlic. Cook for 1 minute. Add the chicken stock, carrots, celery, onion, red bell pepper, paprika, and bay leaf. Lock the lid in place and set the cooker to High pressure for 35 minutes.

4. When the cook time ends, let the pressure release naturally for 10 minutes; manually release any remaining pressure.

5. Carefully remove the lid and remove and discard the bay leaf. Stir in the vinegar.

Ingredient tip: For this recipe, it's important to use the correct variety of paprika. Sweet paprika has a fruity, slightly bitter taste that gives this soup its earthy flavor and vibrant color. If you like things spicy, add 1 tablespoon of hot paprika. But *do not* use smoked paprika here because, with the amount required, the smoke flavor becomes overpowering.

Per Serving: Calories: 342; Total Fat: 24g; Saturated Fat: 7g; Protein: 20g; Total Carbs: 13g; Fiber: 4g; Net Carbs: 9g; Cholesterol: 64mg

DAIRY-FREE, GLUTEN-FREE, NUT-FREE

CLASSIC STUFFED PEPPERS

Prep time: 10 minutes / **Cook time:** 20 minutes

Classic stuffed peppers are one of my favorite comfort foods. Using cauliflower rice instead of white rice adds nutrition and keeps things on the lighter side. Plus, because you don't need to boil the rice first, it shaves off a ton of time to prepare the recipe. Making the peppers in the air fryer also saves time and results in a delicious roasted-pepper flavor. **Serves 4**

2 cups cauliflower rice

1 pound lean ground beef

1 cup Super Simple Marinara (page 132)

¼ cup grated Parmesan cheese

¼ cup fresh parsley, chopped

1 teaspoon Italian seasoning

½ teaspoon garlic powder

Celtic sea salt or kosher salt

Freshly ground black pepper

4 red bell peppers, tops removed, seeded, and ribbed

Olive oil cooking spray, for spritzing

¼ cup shredded part-skim mozzarella cheese, divided

1. In a large bowl, stir together the cauliflower rice, ground beef, marinara, Parmesan, parsley, Italian seasoning, and garlic powder. Season with salt and pepper. Stuff the filling into the peppers. Spritz the peppers and stuffing with cooking spray.

2. Place the stuffed peppers in your air fryer's basket. Fry at 350°F for 15 to 18 minutes, or until the beef is cooked through (it should be at least 160°F when measured with a meat thermometer).

3. Top each pepper with 1 tablespoon of mozzarella cheese and fry again for 1 to 2 minutes to melt the cheese.

Ingredient tip: Red bell peppers are sweeter than green bell peppers, which have a sharp, slightly bitter flavor. For this recipe, look for tall, skinny peppers—they'll fit in the air fryer better than rounder ones.

Per Serving: Calories: 275; Total Fat: 12g; Saturated Fat: 5g; Protein: 29g; Total Carbs: 16g; Fiber: 4g; Net Carbs: 12g; Cholesterol: 81mg

GLUTEN-FREE, NUT-FREE

CORNED BEEF REUBEN CHOWDER

Prep time: 15 minutes / **Cook time:** 30 minutes

This cozy chowder was inspired by one I tried at a local Oktoberfest celebration a few years ago. Sauerkraut gives it the perfect tang, while Swiss cheese and sour cream make it lusciously creamy. I like it best made with leftover corned beef brisket, but deli meat also works—just look for beef that's uncured/nitrate-free. *Serves 6*

1 tablespoon unsalted butter

1 onion, chopped

4 ounces uncured corned beef, thickly sliced and chopped

2 russet potatoes, diced

2 tablespoons all-purpose flour

4 cups Chicken Stock (page 133), or low-sodium store-bought chicken stock

1 cup sauerkraut, drained

¼ cup sour cream

1 cup shredded Swiss cheese

4 scallions, white and green parts, chopped

1. In a Dutch oven over medium heat, melt the butter.

2. Add the onion. Cook for 2 to 3 minutes until softened.

3. Add the corned beef. Cook for 5 minutes, or until the edges begin to curl.

4. Stir in the potatoes. Cook for 2 minutes. Sprinkle in the flour and stir well to combine.

5. Stir in the chicken stock and sauerkraut. Bring the chowder to a simmer. Simmer for 15 minutes, or until the potatoes are cooked through. Remove from the heat.

6. Slowly stir in the sour cream and cheese. Top with the scallions before serving.

Substitution tip: You can substitute fat-free plain Greek yogurt for the sour cream, but it can be temperamental. Instead of stirring it in all at once, add a little bit of warm broth to the yogurt first, to warm it slowly. That way it will be less likely to curdle when added to the pot.

Per Serving: Calories: 222; Total Fat: 10g; Saturated Fat: 6g; Protein: 13g; Total Carbs: 19g; Fiber: 3g; Net Carbs: 16g; Cholesterol: 36mg

NUT-FREE

BAKED SAUSAGE RISOTTO

Prep time: 10 minutes / **Cook time:** 30 minutes

Traditional risotto is great, but it requires a lot of attention and near-constant stirring. This baked version comes out just as creamy, but without the babysitting. Italian-style turkey sausage and kale give the risotto a ton of flavor and transform it into a complete meal. You can use either sweet or hot sausage, depending on your preference. **Serves 4**

1 tablespoon extra-virgin olive oil

8 ounces Italian-style turkey sausage, crumbled

1 onion, diced

3 garlic cloves, minced

¾ cup Arborio rice

2½ cups Chicken Stock (page 133), or low-sodium store-bought chicken stock

¼ cup grated Parmesan cheese

3 cups chopped kale

Celtic sea salt or kosher salt

Freshly ground black pepper

1. Preheat the oven to 425°F.

2. In a Dutch oven over medium-high heat, heat the olive oil.

3. Add the sausage. Cook for 4 to 5 minutes until browned.

4. Stir in the onion and garlic. Cook for 1 to 2 minutes to soften.

5. Stir in the rice, chicken stock, cheese, and kale. Cover the pot and transfer it to the oven. Bake for 20 minutes until the liquid is absorbed and the rice is tender and creamy. Season to taste with salt and pepper.

Leftovers tip: Make a double batch and use the leftovers for baked arancini! Mix the leftover cold risotto with 1 large egg. Form the rice mixture into tablespoon-size balls and roll them in bread crumbs. Bake at 450°F for 20 minutes, or until crispy. Serve with marinara sauce for dipping.

Per Serving: Calories: 289; Total Fat: 7g; Saturated Fat: 2g; Protein: 20g; Total Carbs: 38g; Fiber: 3g; Net Carbs: 35g; Cholesterol: 49mg

GLUTEN-FREE, NUT-FREE

SWEET & SOUR PORK STIR-FRY

Prep time: 10 minutes / **Cook time:** 15 minutes

As a kid, sweet and sour meatballs were one of my favorite dinners. I brought my mom's sweet and sour sauce into the twenty-first century using fresh pineapple and adding ginger and honey. I further transformed it into a stir-fry sauce for easy weeknight dinners. This stir-fry is substantial enough to stand on its own, but is also great served over rice. *Serves 4*

1 tablespoon extra-virgin olive oil

1 tablespoon grated peeled fresh ginger

1 pound pork loin, cut into bite-size pieces

1 cup fresh pineapple chunks, cut into bite-size pieces

1 green bell pepper, cut into bite-size pieces

4 ounces green beans, trimmed

¼ cup apple cider vinegar

2 tablespoons packed light brown sugar

2 tablespoons honey

2 tablespoons low-sodium soy sauce

2 tablespoons cornstarch

1. In a large skillet over medium-high heat, heat the olive oil.

2. Add the ginger. Cook for 1 to 2 minutes until fragrant.

3. Add the pork. Cook for 3 to 4 minutes, stirring frequently, until browned but not cooked through.

4. Stir in the pineapple, green bell pepper, green beans, vinegar, brown sugar, honey, soy sauce, and cornstarch. Bring the mixture to a simmer. Cook for 5 to 7 minutes until the vegetables are soft and the pork is cooked through.

Substitution tip: Use boneless, skinless chicken breast instead of pork loin.

Per Serving: Calories: 302; Total Fat: 12g; Saturated Fat: 4g; Protein: 23g; Total Carbs: 28g; Fiber: 2g; Net Carbs: 26g; Cholesterol: 55mg

DAIRY-FREE, NUT-FREE

AIR-FRIED LAMB MEAT PIES

Prep time: 10 minutes / **Cook time:** 15 minutes

When I was in high school, I was lucky enough to travel to England, Ireland, and Wales. I remember getting back on the bus after a stop and the tour guide was eating something that smelled *amazing*. She told us it was a meat pie called a Cornish pasty. I was determined to get one at our next stop, and they quickly became a favorite. This air-fried version is filled with lamb and turnip, which gives the pies their distinct flavor. **Serves 4**

8 ounces lamb stew meat, finely chopped

½ turnip, finely diced

1 carrot, finely diced

1 shallot, minced

2 tablespoons chopped fresh parsley

½ teaspoon dried thyme

Celtic sea salt or kosher salt

Freshly ground black pepper

1 refrigerated piecrust

1 large egg yolk

1 tablespoon water

1. In a medium bowl, combine the lamb, turnip, carrot, shallot, parsley, and thyme. Generously season with salt and pepper.

2. Cut the piecrust into 4 equal pieces. Spoon the filling into the center of each piece of crust. Fold the dough over the filling to create a wedge shape. Press the edges together tightly to seal the filling inside.

3. In the bowl used for the filling, whisk the egg yolk and water. Brush the egg wash on the pastry. Place the pies in your air fryer's basket. Fry at 350°F for 12 minutes, or until golden brown and flaky.

4. Let the meat pies cool for 10 minutes before serving—the inside will be very hot.

Ingredient tip: I love the flavor of lamb, but use beef sirloin if you prefer.

Per Serving: Calories: 268; Total Fat: 15g; Saturated Fat: 3g; Protein: 14g; Total Carbs: 19g; Fiber: 2g; Net Carbs: 17g; Cholesterol: 91mg

NUT-FREE, DAIRY-FREE

BARBECUE MEATLOAF & MASHED POTATOES

Prep time: 10 minutes / **Cook time:** 30 minutes

I always forget how easy it is to make meatloaf. To turn this classic comfort food meal into a one-pot recipe, I wrap potatoes in aluminum foil and steam them on the same sheet pan. The resulting mashed potatoes are so creamy you won't believe they came out of the oven. **Serves 4**

Olive oil cooking spray

1 pound small red potatoes, quartered

¼ cup water

12 ounces lean ground beef

1 large egg

¼ cup plain bread crumbs

1 teaspoon steak seasoning

½ teaspoon onion powder

¼ cup Maple Barbecue Sauce (page 136), or your favorite store-bought barbecue sauce

12 ounces green beans, trimmed

Celtic sea salt or kosher salt

Freshly ground black pepper

1 tablespoon unsalted butter

½ cup fat-free plain Greek yogurt

1. Preheat the oven to 425°F.

2. Coat a 12-inch-long piece of foil with cooking spray. Place the potatoes on the foil and drizzle them with the water. Fold the foil up around the potatoes, sealing them tightly, and place the packet on a sheet pan.

3. In a large bowl, combine the ground beef, egg, bread crumbs, steak seasoning, and onion powder. Gently mix to combine. Form the meat mixture in an 8-by-4-inch loaf on the other side of the sheet pan. Spread the barbecue sauce over the meatloaf. Bake for 15 minutes.

4. Add the green beans to the pan. Spritz with cooking spray and season with salt and pepper. Bake for 15 minutes more.

5. Carefully unwrap the potatoes, forming a bowl out of the foil. Add the butter and yogurt to the potatoes. Using a potato masher or heavy wooden spoon, mash the potatoes. Season to taste with salt and pepper.

Make-ahead tip: Mix the meatloaf mixture up to 1 day ahead and keep it refrigerated. Add 5 to 10 minutes to the cooking time.

Per Serving: Calories: 376; Total Fat: 12g; Saturated Fat: 6g; Protein: 32g; Total Carbs: 35g; Fiber: 3g; Net Carbs: 32g; Cholesterol: 116mg

---

NUT-FREE

PORK & GREEN BEAN STIR-FRY

Prep time: 10 minutes / **Cook time:** 15 minutes

One fall weekend a few years ago, we were looking for something fun to do and randomly ended up at a garlic festival in Vermont. It was fantastic, and we've returned almost every year since. This garlicky stir-fry was inspired by the sauce they spoon over spicy pork dumplings. I usually make it with noodles, but using cauliflower rice instead means it can be made in one pan and you can use less pork. **Serves 4**

¼ cup Chicken Stock (page 133), or low-sodium store-bought chicken stock

2 tablespoons low-sodium soy sauce

1 tablespoon rice vinegar

1 to 2 tablespoons sambal oelek (chili paste)

2 teaspoons sesame oil

1 tablespoon extra-virgin olive oil

4 large garlic cloves, minced

1 tablespoon grated peeled fresh ginger

8 ounces lean ground pork

2 cups cauliflower rice

8 ounces green beans, trimmed

1. In a small bowl, stir together the chicken stock, soy sauce, vinegar, sambal oelek, and sesame oil. Set aside.

2. In a large skillet over medium-high heat, heat the olive oil.

3. Add the garlic and ginger. Cook for 2 to 3 minutes until they begin to soften.

4. Add the ground pork. Cook for 5 minutes, stirring occasionally, or until nearly cooked through.

5. Stir in the cauliflower rice, green beans, and sauce. Bring to a simmer. Cook for 5 to 7 minutes until the pork is cooked through.

Substitution tip: You can make this recipe gluten-free if you use tamari or coconut aminos instead of soy sauce. It'll still taste great, but won't have the same depth of flavor that soy sauce provides.

Per Serving: Calories: 201; Total Fat: 13g; Saturated Fat: 3g; Protein: 14g; Total Carbs: 9g; Fiber: 3g; Net Carbs: 6g; Cholesterol: 37mg

DAIRY-FREE, NUT-FREE

TACO CASSEROLE

Prep time: 10 minutes / **Cook time:** 25 minutes

Taco casserole is one of the most popular recipes on my blog, so I felt like I had to adapt it to a one-pot version for this book! In the original version, I bake the casserole over a bed of tortilla chips. This version is made entirely on the stovetop and is almost more of a chili that you can scoop up with the chips. I also add big chunks of zucchini for extra texture and flavor. **Serves 6**

1 tablespoon extra-virgin olive oil

1 onion, chopped

2 garlic cloves, minced

1 pound lean ground beef

2 tablespoons taco seasoning

1 zucchini, cut into 1-inch pieces

1 (15.5-ounce) can low-sodium black beans, drained

1 cup salsa

1 cup shredded Cheddar or Mexican blend cheese

1 avocado, sliced (optional)

6 ounces corn tortilla chips

1. In a Dutch oven over medium-high heat, heat the olive oil.

2. Add the onion and garlic. Cook for 2 to 3 minutes until softened.

3. Add the ground beef and taco seasoning. Cook for about 5 minutes, stirring frequently, until browned.

4. Stir in the zucchini, black beans, and salsa. Simmer the mixture for 10 minutes.

5. Top with the cheese. Cover the pot and cook for 3 to 4 minutes until the cheese melts.

6. Top with the avocado (if using). Serve with the tortilla chips.

Substitution tip: For a lighter version, use ground chicken or turkey breast instead of beef.

Per Serving: Calories: 392; Total Fat: 16g; Saturated Fat: 7g; Protein: 27g; Total Carbs: 37g; Fiber: 8g; Net Carbs: 29g; Cholesterol: 70mg

NUT-FREE

PAN-ROASTED PORK CHOPS WITH GRAPES

Prep time: 10 minutes / **Cook time:** 20 to 25 minutes

I have a thing for roasted grapes. They come out warm and jammy, and aren't as sweet as you'd expect them to be. For this recipe, I pair them with pork chops and quinoa for an easy one-pot meal that's full of savory flavor. Sear the pork chops on the stovetop and finish the cooking in the oven. Serves 4

---

4 (½-inch-thick) bone-in pork loin chops

Celtic sea salt or kosher salt

Freshly ground black pepper

1 tablespoon extra-virgin olive oil

2 cups Chicken Stock (page 133), or low-sodium store-bought chicken stock

1 shallot, thinly sliced

1 teaspoon chopped fresh rosemary

¼ teaspoon dried thyme

1 cup quinoa, any color, rinsed well

2 cups seedless red grapes, halved

1. Preheat the oven to 400°F.

2. Season the pork chops with salt and pepper.

3. In a large ovenproof skillet over high heat, heat the olive oil.

4. Add the pork chops. Cook for 1 to 2 minutes per side until browned.

5. Stir in the chicken stock, shallot, rosemary, thyme, quinoa, and grapes. Transfer the skillet to the oven and bake for 15 minutes.

6. Transfer the pork chops to a plate and let rest. If the quinoa needs more time, return the skillet to the oven for 5 minutes more.

Substitution tip: For a Middle Eastern twist, swap the quinoa for couscous and use 1½ cups of stock. Keep in mind the recipe will no longer be gluten-free.

Per Serving: Calories: 409; Total Fat: 15g; Saturated Fat: 4g; Protein: 30g; Total Carbs: 36g; Fiber: 5g; Net Carbs: 31g; Cholesterol: 64mg

---

DAIRY-FREE, GLUTEN-FREE, NUT-FREE

ROASTED EGGPLANT WITH GROUND LAMB

Prep time: 10 minutes / **Cook time:** 50 minutes

This simple lamb and eggplant recipe is one I crave frequently. Coriander gives it a warm, earthy flavor that pairs really well with the lamb. Briny feta and fresh parsley brighten the flavors and keep it from tasting too heavy. This meal is delicious on its own, but I also love it served with fresh pita bread and quick cucumber pickles (see page 122). **Serves 6**

---

1 tablespoon extra-virgin olive oil

2 garlic cloves, minced

1 pound ground lamb

2 teaspoons ground coriander

1 large (about 1½ pounds) globe eggplant, peeled and cut into 1-inch cubes

3 cups grape tomatoes, halved

1 tablespoon tomato paste

½ cup water

2 ounces feta cheese, crumbled

2 tablespoons chopped fresh parsley

1. Preheat the oven to 400°F.

2. In a Dutch oven over medium-high heat, heat the olive oil.

3. Add the garlic. Cook for 1 to 2 minutes until fragrant.

4. Crumble in the lamb and sprinkle in the coriander. Cook for 5 to 7 minutes, stirring occasionally, until browned.

5. Stir in the eggplant, tomatoes, tomato paste, and water. Transfer the pot to the oven and cook, uncovered, for 30 to 40 minutes until the vegetables are very soft and the liquid has cooked off.

6. Sprinkle with the cheese and parsley before serving.

Substitution tip: If you have it in your spice rack, swap the coriander for ras el hanout, a delicious North African blend of ginger, nutmeg, turmeric, and other warm spices.

Per Serving: Calories: 298; Total Fat: 23g; Saturated Fat: 10g; Protein: 16g; Total Carbs: 9g; Fiber: 4g; Net Carbs: 5g; Cholesterol: 65mg

---

GLUTEN-FREE, NUT-FREE

BARBECUE BAKED RIBS

Prep time: 10 minutes / **Cook time:** 1 hour

This easy sheet pan dinner packs a ton of flavor with minimal effort. Rubbing the pork with smoked paprika before baking imparts a smoky, grill-like flavor. For the crispiest sweet potato fries, don't skip the cornstarch and don't salt the potatoes before they're fully cooked. **Serves 4**

1½ pounds boneless country-style pork ribs

1 tablespoon smoked paprika

2 sweet potatoes, cut into ¼-inch sticks

1 tablespoon cornstarch

1 tablespoon extra-virgin olive oil

¼ cup Maple Barbecue Sauce (page 136)

1 pound green beans, trimmed

Celtic sea salt or kosher salt

Freshly ground black pepper

1. Preheat the oven to 375°F. Line a sheet pan with heavy-duty aluminum foil.

2. Rub the ribs with the paprika and arrange them on one side of the prepared sheet pan.

3. In a medium bowl, toss the sweet potato fries with the cornstarch. Drizzle them with the olive oil and arrange the coated sweet potatoes in a single layer on the other side of the sheet pan. Bake for 45 minutes until the ribs are tender and cooked through.

4. Brush the ribs with barbecue sauce. Add the green beans to the pan. Season the green beans and sweet potato fries with salt and pepper. Bake for 15 minutes more until the vegetables are soft and the sauce is nicely caramelized.

Ingredient tip: Country style ribs aren't actually ribs at all—they're cut from the loin, near the shoulder. They're meatier than baby back ribs or spare ribs.

Per Serving: Calories: 495; Total Fat: 30g; Saturated Fat: 9g; Protein: 27g; Total Carbs: 30g; Fiber: 7g; Net Carbs: 23g; Cholesterol: 94mg

DAIRY-FREE, GLUTEN-FREE, NUT-FREE

PORK EGG ROLL IN A BOWL

Prep time: 5 minutes / **Cook time:** 15 minutes

Egg rolls are my favorite part of Chinese take-out, but with this recipe for "egg roll in a bowl" you won't miss them. Once you ditch the deep-fried wrapper, egg rolls are actually surprisingly healthy. This recipe combines shredded cabbage and ground pork—classic egg roll flavors—with fragrant spices such as ginger and sambal oelek for a deconstructed egg roll you can eat with a fork. **Serves 4**

1 tablespoon sesame oil

4 garlic cloves, minced

1 teaspoon grated peeled fresh ginger

8 ounces ground pork

2 tablespoons low-sodium soy sauce

1 tablespoon sambal oelek

1 tablespoon rice vinegar

6 cups coleslaw mix

5 scallions, white and green parts, sliced

1. In a large skillet over medium-high heat, heat the sesame oil.

2. Add the garlic and ginger. Cook for 2 to 3 minutes until fragrant.

3. Add the ground pork. Cook for 7 to 10 minutes, breaking up the meat with a spoon, until browned and cooked through.

4. Stir in the soy sauce, sambal oelek, and vinegar. Cook for 1 minute until the liquid is nearly evaporated.

5. Stir in the coleslaw mix. Cook for 2 to 3 minutes until wilted.

6. Stir in the scallions.

Substitution tip: For a leaner option, use ground turkey breast instead of pork.

Per Serving: Calories: 163; Total Fat: 9g; Saturated Fat: 3g; Protein: 13g; Total Carbs: 9g; Fiber: 3g; Net Carbs: 6g; Cholesterol: 42mg

DAIRY-FREE, NUT-FREE

PRESSURE COOKER BOLOGNESE WITH SPAGHETTI SQUASH

Prep time: 15 minutes / **Time to pressure:** 10 minutes / **Cook time:** 15 to 20 minutes / **Release time:** 5 minutes

Bolognese, a rich, meaty sauce finished with a swirl of cream, takes hours to make on the stovetop. Making it in a pressure cooker, however, means you can make it in under 1 hour, but it still has that rich, simmered-all-day flavor. I add spaghetti squash right to the pot so it can cook along with the sauce. This will be very hot when it's done, so let it cool before you dig in. **Serves 4**

4 ounces pancetta, chopped

2 celery stalks, chopped

2 carrots, grated

1 onion, minced

1 pound lean ground beef

2 cups Super Simple Marinara (page 132)

2 bay leaves

1 spaghetti squash, cut crosswise into 4 rings, seeded

½ cup half-and-half

¼ cup chopped fresh parsley

1. On your pressure cooker, select Sauté. Put the pancetta into the cooker. Cook for 2 to 3 minutes, stirring once or twice, or until crisp.

2. Add the celery, carrots, onion, ground beef, marinara, and bay leaves. Place the squash rings over the sauce. Lock the lid in place and set the cooker to High pressure for 12 minutes.

3. When the cook time ends, manually release the pressure.

4. Carefully remove the lid and the squash rings from the pot. Stir in the half-and-half and parsley. For a thicker sauce, select Sauté and cook, uncovered, for 5 minutes more.

5. To serve, spoon the sauce over the squash rings.

Ingredient tip: Most people cut spaghetti squash lengthwise, which can be very difficult. Cutting it crosswise into rings is much easier—plus it results in longer strands of "spaghetti."

Per Serving: Calories: 386; Total Fat: 20g; Saturated Fat: 8g; Protein: 32g; Total Carbs: 21g; Fiber: 3g; Net Carbs: 19g; Cholesterol: 101mg

GLUTEN-FREE, NUT-FREE

CARNE ASADA TACOS

Prep time: 10 minutes / **Cook time:** 15 minutes

I've never met a taco I didn't like, but one of my favorite ways to enjoy them is with grilled steak and a simple onion and cilantro salsa. Carne asada is usually grilled, but the beef also comes out surprisingly well in the air fryer—the edges get nicely charred while the inside stays tender and juicy. **Serves 4**

FOR THE CARNE ASADA

1 tablespoon extra-virgin olive oil

1 tablespoon distilled white vinegar

2 garlic cloves, minced

½ teaspoon ground cumin

Celtic sea salt or kosher salt

Freshly ground black pepper

1 pound flank steak

FOR THE TACOS

1 onion, diced

¼ cup fresh cilantro, chopped

Juice of 1 lime

1 jalapeño pepper, minced (optional)

Celtic sea salt or kosher salt

12 gluten-free corn tortillas

1 avocado, sliced

TO MAKE THE CARNE ASADA

1. In a large bowl, whisk the olive oil, vinegar, garlic, and cumin. Season to taste with salt and pepper. Add the steak to the bowl and turn to coat. Let marinate for at least 10 minutes, or up to overnight, covered.

2. Put the steak in your air fryer's basket. Fry at 370°F for 10 to 12 minutes until deeply browned and cooked to your desired level of doneness. Remove and finely chop the steak.

TO MAKE THE TACOS

1. While the steak cooks, in a small bowl, stir together the onion, cilantro, lime juice, and jalapeño (if using). Season to taste with salt. Mix well.

2. To serve, spoon the steak onto the tortillas. Top with the salsa and avocado.

Substitution tip: Flank steak is my favorite, but it can sometimes be hard to find. Substitute top round in a pinch.

Per Serving: Calories: 445; Total Fat: 19g; Saturated Fat: 5g; Protein: 30g; Total Carbs: 39g; Fiber: 8g; Net Carbs: 31g; Cholesterol: 50mg

DAIRY-FREE, GLUTEN-FREE, NUT-FREE

SLOW COOKER BEEF STEW

Prep time: 15 minutes / **Cook time:** 8 hours

Beef stew is the quintessential slow cooker recipe—cooking low and slow results in tender meat and vegetables blanketed in a rich, creamy gravy. Red wine and tomato paste add a little acidity and keep the flavors from tasting muddy. The parsley added at the end contributes a pop of freshness. Serve this stew with a chunk of crusty bread and get excited for leftovers—this stew tastes even better the next day. **Serves 6**

2 pounds chuck roast, trimmed and cut into 1-inch pieces

¼ cup white whole-wheat flour

Celtic sea salt or kosher salt

Freshly ground black pepper

4 garlic cloves, smashed

6 carrots, sliced

3 red potatoes, diced

1 onion, chopped

2 cups low-sodium beef stock, or Garden Vegetable Stock (page 135), or low-sodium store-bought vegetable stock

½ cup red wine (optional)

2 tablespoons tomato paste

¼ cup fresh parsley, chopped

1. In your slow cooker, combine the beef and flour. Stir to coat. Generously season with salt and pepper.

2. Add the garlic, carrots, potatoes, onion, stock, red wine (if using), and tomato paste. Cover the cooker and set it to low heat. Cook for 8 hours, or until the beef is very tender.

3. Stir in the parsley and adjust the seasoning to taste.

Substitution tip: Beef stew is incredibly versatile. Try it with whatever root vegetables you like, just keep the total amount to about 6 cups. I love adding parsnips and turnips.

Per Serving: Calories: 382; Total Fat: 10g; Saturated Fat: 4g; Protein: 41g; Total Carbs: 31g; Fiber: 4g; Net Carbs: 27g; Cholesterol: 114mg

DAIRY-FREE, NUT-FREE

SLOW COOKER CABBAGE ROLL SOUP

Prep time: 5 minutes / **Cook time:** 8 to 10 hours

I love cabbage rolls, but they're a major pain to make. Skip the boiling, rolling, and steaming and throw everything into the slow cooker to make an easy soup instead! It has all the flavor of traditional rolls without the fuss. The barley will continue to soak up the broth as it sits, so you might want to add a little water or broth if you're reheating leftovers. **Serves 6**

1 head green
    cabbage, shredded

4 cups Chicken Stock
    (page 133), or low-sodium
    store-bought chicken stock

2 cups Super Simple Marinara
    (page 132)

½ cup barley

2 carrots, shredded

1 onion, chopped

1 celery stalk, minced

1 parsnip, shredded

1 pound lean ground beef

2 tablespoons apple
    cider vinegar

Celtic sea salt or kosher salt

Freshly ground black pepper

In your slow cooker, combine the cabbage, chicken stock, marinara, barley, carrots, onion, celery, parsnip, ground beef, and vinegar. Stir well to combine, breaking up the beef. Cover the cooker and set it to low heat. Cook for 8 to 10 hours. Season to taste with salt and pepper.

Ingredient tip: I love barley's chewy texture and nutty flavor, but it isn't gluten-free. If you need to, substitute parboiled rice.

Per Serving: Calories: 234; Total Fat: 6g; Saturated Fat: 2g; Protein: 20g; Total Carbs: 27g; Fiber: 8g; Net Carbs: 19g; Cholesterol: 47mg

DAIRY-FREE, NUT-FREE

SLOW COOKER PULLED PORK

Prep time: 5 minutes / **Cook time:** 8 hours

Slow cookers are great for making saucy recipes like pulled pork that cook all day long. I use pork loin, which is leaner than the traditional pork shoulder, and rub it with smoked paprika to mimic the flavor of a long, slow smoke. Serve this shredded pork on whole-grain rolls with vinegar slaw. If I have pickles in the fridge, I also like to slip a few into my sandwich. **Serves 6**

3 pounds boneless pork loin

1 tablespoon smoked paprika

1 teaspoon dry mustard

Celtic sea salt or kosher salt

Freshly ground black pepper

2 cups Chicken Stock
(page 133), or low-sodium
store-bought chicken stock

½ cup apple cider vinegar

3 tablespoons tomato paste

2 cups shredded cabbage

Juice of 1 lime

¼ cup fresh cilantro, chopped

6 whole-grain rolls

1. Rub the pork loin all over with paprika and mustard. Season with salt and pepper. Place the pork in your slow cooker. Pour in the chicken stock and vinegar. Add the tomato paste. Cover the cooker and set it to low heat. Cook for 8 hours until the pork shreds easily.

2. Remove the pork and shred it. Return it to the pot for 10 minutes so it soaks up more sauce.

3. In a medium bowl, stir together the cabbage, lime juice, and cilantro. Season to taste with salt.

4. Divide the pork among the roll bottoms. Top with slaw and cover with the top buns.

Substitution tip: You can also make this recipe with boneless, skinless chicken breasts instead of pork.

Per Serving: Calories: 425; Total Fat: 12g; Saturated Fat: 3g; Protein: 53g; Total Carbs: 23g; Fiber: 4g; Net Carbs: 19g; Cholesterol: 140mg

DAIRY-FREE, NUT-FREE

Chapter 6

SEAFOOD

RED CURRY SALMON WITH VEGETABLES

Prep time: 10 minutes / **Cook time:** 10 minutes

Air fryers and salmon are made for each other—the skin comes out perfectly crispy and the fish doesn't dry out like it can when you bake it in the oven. For this recipe, I spread the salmon with red curry paste and coconut milk and roast it over a bed of asparagus and bell pepper for a flavorful meal. **Serves 4**

1 tablespoon red curry paste

1 tablespoon full-fat coconut milk

1 teaspoon freshly squeezed lime juice

4 (5-ounce) salmon fillets

1 pound asparagus, woody ends trimmed

1 red bell pepper, sliced

Celtic sea salt or kosher salt

Freshly ground black pepper

Olive oil cooking spray, for preparing the vegetables

1. In a small bowl, stir together the curry paste, coconut milk, and lime juice to form a smooth paste. Spread the curry paste over the salmon skin.

2. In your air fryer's basket, combine the asparagus and red bell pepper. Season with salt and pepper. Spritz the vegetables with cooking spray.

3. Place the salmon, skin-side up, on top of the vegetables. Fry at 375°F for 5 to 8 minutes until the salmon is cooked through and flakes easily with a fork.

Ingredient tip: Red curry paste is a flavorful mixture of lemongrass, ginger, and red chiles and is a common ingredient in Thai food.

Per Serving: Calories: 246; Total Fat: 11g; Saturated Fat: 3g; Protein: 30g; Total Carbs: 9g; Fiber: 3g; Net Carbs: 6g; Cholesterol: 75mg

DAIRY-FREE, GLUTEN-FREE

MUSSELS PROVENÇAL

Prep time: 10 minutes / **Cook time:** 15 minutes

This recipe was inspired by one of my go-to orders at one of our favorite cafés. Mussels are light, so they're usually served with something else—like fries—to fill you up. This recipe is full of hearty vegetables, such as mushrooms and peppers, so all you need is a little bread to help you sop up every last bit of broth. **Serves 4**

2 tablespoons extra-virgin olive oil

1 fennel bulb, cored, white part thinly sliced

1 pint mushrooms, sliced

4 garlic cloves, minced

1 shallot, minced

1 tomato, diced

1 green bell pepper, sliced

2 tablespoons water

3 pounds mussels, scrubbed well

1 whole-grain baguette (optional)

1. In a Dutch oven over medium-high heat, heat the olive oil.

2. Add the fennel, mushrooms, garlic, and shallot. Cook for 4 to 5 minutes, stirring occasionally, until softened.

3. Stir in the tomato, green bell pepper, and water. Cook for 4 to 5 minutes more, stirring occasionally, or until the tomato begins to break down into a sauce.

4. Add the mussels. Cover the pot and cook for 5 to 7 minutes, or until the mussels open. Discard any mussels that do not open.

5. Serve with the baguette for sopping (if using).

Substitution tip: Mussels are easy to cook at home, but they can be intimidating. If you don't want to make them—or if you're just not in the mood—swap them for 1 pound of peeled, deveined shrimp.

Per Serving: Calories: 253; Total Fat: 11g; Saturated Fat: 2g; Protein: 23g; Total Carbs: 16g; Fiber: 3g; Net Carbs: 13g; Cholesterol: 48mg

DAIRY-FREE, NUT-FREE

SHRIMP TACO BOWLS

Prep time: 10 minutes / **Cook time:** 7 minutes

Taco night is my favorite, but, when I make tacos, I always end up eating too many. Luckily, I've found that if I pile the ingredients into a bowl instead—and eat them with a fork instead of my fingers—I'm satisfied with a much more reasonable portion. Instead of making these bowls with rice, I pile the toppings on a bed of citrusy cabbage slaw to keep things on the lighter side. **Serves 4**

FOR THE SHRIMP

1 teaspoon extra-virgin
   olive oil

1 pound fresh shrimp, peeled
   and deveined

1 tablespoon gluten-free
   chili powder

FOR THE BOWLS

2 cups coleslaw mix

Juice of 1 lime

2 teaspoons extra-virgin
   olive oil

Celtic sea salt or kosher salt

¼ cup canned low-sodium
   black beans, rinsed
   and drained, or cooked
   black beans

1 cup diced fresh pineapple

½ small red onion, minced

1 jalapeño pepper, minced

¼ cup fresh cilantro, chopped

1 avocado, sliced

2 ounces corn tortilla
   chips (optional)

TO MAKE THE SHRIMP

1. In a large skillet over medium-high heat, heat the olive oil.

2. Sprinkle the shrimp with the chili powder and add them to the hot oil. Sauté for 5 to 7 minutes, or until opaque and cooked through.

TO MAKE THE BOWLS

1. In a large bowl, combine the coleslaw mix, lime juice, and olive oil. Mix well. Season to taste with salt. Divide the slaw among 4 bowls.

2. Top the slaw with the shrimp, black beans, pineapple, red onion, jalapeño, cilantro, and avocado. Serve with tortilla chips (if using).

Repurpose tip: The mixture of pineapple, onion, cilantro, and jalapeño in this recipe makes a delicious salsa. Make extra and spoon it over chicken or fish, or eat it on tortilla chips.

Per Serving: Calories: 246; Total Fat: 11g; Saturated Fat: 2g; Protein: 24g; Total Carbs: 18g; Fiber: 6g; Net Carbs: 12g; Cholesterol: 160mg

DAIRY-FREE, GLUTEN-FREE, NUT-FREE

FISH & CHIPS

Prep time: 10 minutes / **Cook time:** 15 minutes

Fish and chips was one of the first recipes I made when I bought my air fryer. The breading comes out nice and crispy without any greasy oil and the fish stays tender and flaky. To keep this meal on the lighter side, I fill my plate with an easy citrus slaw that comes together quickly while the fish cooks. **Serves 4**

FOR THE FISH AND CHIPS

2 large eggs, lightly beaten

½ cup plain bread crumbs

4 (4-ounce) tilapia or haddock fillets

All-purpose flour

Celtic sea salt or kosher salt

Freshly ground black pepper

Olive oil cooking spray

2 russet potatoes, cut into ¼-inch planks

1 tablespoon extra-virgin olive oil

TO MAKE THE FISH AND CHIPS

1. Place the beaten eggs in a shallow bowl and the bread crumbs in a second shallow bowl.

2. Sprinkle the fish with flour and season with salt and pepper. Dredge the fillets in the egg, remove, and coat with the bread crumbs. Spritz the coated fillets with cooking spray.

3. In a large bowl, toss the potato planks with the olive oil. Place the potatoes in your air fryer's basket and top with the breaded fish. Fry at 375°F for 15 minutes, turning halfway through the cooking time, until the fish is cooked through (when the thickest part is cut into, it will be opaque and flake easily with a fork).

FOR THE SLAW

2 cups coleslaw mix

1 tablespoon extra-virgin olive oil

Juice of 1 lime

4 radishes, thinly sliced

1 shallot, thinly sliced

2 tablespoons chopped fresh cilantro

Celtic sea salt or kosher salt

Freshly ground black pepper

TO MAKE THE SLAW

In a medium bowl, combine the coleslaw mix, olive oil, lime juice, radishes, shallot, and cilantro. Mix well. Season to taste with salt and pepper. Set aside until serving.

Repurpose tip: This citrusy slaw is a great way to add crunch to a Slow Cooker Pulled Pork (page 90) sandwich.

Per Serving: Calories: 366; Total Fat: 13g; Saturated Fat: 3g; Protein: 29g; Total Carbs: 34g; Fiber: 4g; Net Carbs: 30g; Cholesterol: 148mg

DAIRY-FREE, NUT-FREE

PRESSURE COOKER CIOPPINO

- -

Prep time: 5 minutes / **Time to pressure:** 15 minutes / **Cook time:** 7 minutes / **Release time:** 10 minutes

- -

I won my very first cooking contest with a cioppino recipe similar to this one, so it only seems right to share one here. I updated this recipe to be made in a pressure cooker, swapping shellfish, like mussels, for frozen shrimp and scallops. I love adding a pinch of saffron to my broth—it goes so well with tomatoes and makes this seafood stew extra special. **Serves 4**

- -

1 tablespoon extra-virgin
  olive oil

2 celery stalks, minced

1 onion, minced

1 green bell pepper, minced

2 garlic cloves, thinly sliced

4 cups Super Simple Marinara
  (page 132)

1¼ cups low-sodium fish stock

1 teaspoon dried oregano

Generous pinch
  saffron threads

1 pound frozen
  medium shrimp

1 pound frozen scallops

2 tablespoons chopped
  fresh parsley

Celtic sea salt or kosher salt

Freshly ground black pepper

1. On your pressure cooker, select Sauté. Pour in the olive oil to heat.

2. Add the celery, onion, green bell pepper, and garlic. Cook for 3 to 4 minutes to soften.

3. Stir in the marinara, fish stock, oregano, and saffron threads. Add the shrimp and scallops. Lock the lid in place and set the cooker to High pressure for 3 minutes.

4. When the cook time ends, let the pressure release naturally for 10 minutes; manually release any remaining pressure.

5. Carefully remove the lid and top the cioppino with parsley. Season to taste with salt and pepper.

- -

Make-ahead tip: This stew is even tastier the next day; make it ahead and gently reheat until warmed through.

Per Serving: Calories: 309; Total Fat: 8g; Saturated Fat: 2g; Protein: 53g; Total Carbs: 10g; Fiber: 2g; Net Carbs: 8g; Cholesterol: 277mg

- -

DAIRY-FREE, GLUTEN-FREE, NUT-FREE

SHRIMP & SAUSAGE PAELLA

Prep time: 5 minutes / **Cook time:** 35 minutes

Restaurant paella can cost a small fortune, but it's easy to make at home. This scaled-down version uses shrimp and sausage, but you can add any shellfish you like. Don't stir it too much while it cooks. The key to a great paella is to let the rice at the bottom of the pan form a toasty crust known as *socarrat*. **Serves 4**

1 tablespoon extra-virgin olive oil

1 onion, chopped

1 red bell pepper, chopped

4 ounces chicken chorizo, diced

2 cups long-grain white rice

5 cups Chicken Stock (page 133), or low-sodium store-bought chicken stock

Generous pinch saffron threads

1 pound fresh shrimp, peeled and deveined

1 cup peas, fresh or frozen

¼ cup fresh parsley

Juice of 1 lemon

Celtic sea salt or kosher salt

1. In a large skillet over medium heat, heat the olive oil.

2. When the oil is hot, add the onion and red bell pepper. Sauté for 3 to 5 minutes to soften.

3. Add the chorizo. Cook for 5 minutes to brown.

4. Stir in the rice, chicken stock, and saffron threads. Cook for 20 minutes, or until most of the stock is absorbed and the rice is soft.

5. Add the shrimp and peas. Cook for 5 minutes, or until the shrimp are opaque and cooked through.

6. Stir in the parsley and lemon juice. Season to taste with salt.

Ingredient tip: Saffron has a sweet, floral flavor and bright yellow color that transforms whatever you put it in. It's known for being pricey, but a little goes a long way and it's easy to find small packages for just a few dollars. No saffron? Substitute turmeric.

Per Serving: Calories: 605; Total Fat: 9g; Saturated Fat: 2g; Protein: 41g; Total Carbs: 88g; Fiber: 4g; Net Carbs: 84g; Cholesterol: 219mg

DAIRY-FREE, GLUTEN-FREE, NUT-FREE

MANHATTAN CLAM CHOWDER

Prep time: 15 minutes / **Cook time:** 25 minutes

I have loved clam chowder since I was a kid. Homemade chowder is surprisingly easy to make and tastes so much better than canned versions. Bacon adds a subtle smoky element that I love, but you can leave it out, if you prefer. My favorite way to serve this soup is with some crusty bread and a dash or two of hot sauce! *Serves 4*

4 sugar-free bacon slices, chopped

1 onion, diced

4 garlic cloves, minced

2 celery stalks, diced

2 carrots, diced

1 teaspoon dried oregano

1 (14.5-ounce) can diced fire-roasted tomatoes

2 red potatoes, diced

1 cup Chicken Stock (page 133), or low-sodium store-bought chicken stock

1 (10-ounce) can baby clams

Juice of 1 lemon

Celtic sea salt or kosher salt

Freshly ground black pepper

1. In a Dutch oven over high heat, fry the bacon for 5 minutes, or until crispy. Turn the heat to low.

2. Add the onion, garlic, celery, carrots, and oregano. Cook for 5 minutes, stirring occasionally, until the vegetables begin to soften.

3. Add the tomatoes, potatoes, chicken stock, and clams. Bring the chowder to a simmer. Cook for about 15 minutes until the potatoes and carrots are soft.

4. Remove from the heat and stir in the lemon juice. Season to taste with salt and pepper.

Ingredient tip: Baby clams are smaller and more tender than chopped clams, although you can also use those, if you prefer.

Per Serving: Calories: 200; Total Fat: 9g; Saturated Fat: 3g; Protein: 18g; Total Carbs: 12g; Fiber: 3g; Net Carbs: 9g; Cholesterol: 63mg

DAIRY-FREE, GLUTEN-FREE, NUT-FREE

SHEET PAN LEMON-HERB TUNA WITH GNOCCHI

Prep time: 10 minutes / **Cook time:** 25 minutes

Sheet pan gnocchi is one of my favorite weeknight cooking tricks. These potato dumplings cook up crispy on the outside and fluffy on the inside—no boiling required. For this recipe, I roast the gnocchi with zucchini and serve it with lemon-herb tuna steaks that cook on the same pan. **Serves 4**

4 (4-ounce) tuna steaks
½ teaspoon dried oregano
½ teaspoon dried thyme
1 lemon, sliced
1 pound dry gnocchi
1 zucchini, diced
1 tablespoon extra-virgin
   olive oil
Celtic sea salt or kosher salt
Freshly ground black pepper

1. Preheat the oven to 450°F.

2. Place the tuna steaks on one side of a sheet pan. Rub each with the oregano and thyme. Place 1 lemon slice on top of each tuna steak.

3. Spread the gnocchi and zucchini over the rest of the pan, breaking up any pieces of gnocchi that are stuck together. Drizzle with the olive oil and mix to coat. Season with salt and pepper.

4. Bake for 20 to 25 minutes until the gnocchi are soft and the tuna is cooked to your liking.

Ingredient tip: Gnocchi are small dumplings made primarily from potatoes. Look for them near the pasta.

Per Serving: Calories: 347; Total Fat: 7g; Saturated Fat: 1g; Protein: 34g; Total Carbs: 37g; Fiber: 4g; Net Carbs: 33g; Cholesterol: 32mg

DAIRY-FREE, NUT-FREE

PRESSURE COOKER SHRIMP BOIL

Prep time: 5 minutes / **Time to pressure:** 15 minutes / **Cook time:** 1 minute / **Release time:** 10 minutes

This shrimp boil is hands-down one of my favorite pressure cooker recipes. The potatoes come out amazingly tender and the shrimp come out perfectly—it's almost like magic! A little hot sauce gives this recipe classic flavor without adding too much heat. Add more at the table if you like things on the spicier side. *Serves 4*

1 pound baby red
potatoes, halved

2 andouille links, sliced

1 cup Chicken Stock
(page 133), or low-sodium
store-bought chicken stock

4 ears fresh corn, shucked and
halved crosswise

1 tablespoon reduced-sodium
Old Bay seasoning

1 tablespoon hot sauce

1 pound frozen (large)
peel-and-eat shrimp

1 tablespoon unsalted butter

¼ cup fresh parsley leaves

1 lemon, cut into wedges

1. In your pressure cooker, combine the potatoes, sausage, chicken stock, corn, seasoning, hot sauce, and shrimp. Lock the lid in place and set the cooker to High pressure for 1 minute.

2. When the cook time ends, let the pressure release naturally for 10 minutes; manually release any remaining pressure.

3. Carefully remove the lid and stir in the butter and parsley. Serve with the lemon wedges for squeezing.

Ingredient tip: Using frozen shrimp in this recipe makes it easy, but the longer cooking time also means they won't overcook.

Per Serving: Calories: 401; Total Fat: 11g; Saturated Fat: 4g; Protein: 40g; Total Carbs: 35g; Fiber: 5g; Net Carbs: 30g; Cholesterol: 211mg

GLUTEN-FREE, NUT-FREE

OVEN-BLACKENED TILAPIA

Prep time: 10 minutes / **Cook time:** 15 minutes

This blackened tilapia is great when you want dinner on the lighter side and don't feel like cooking. The fish has a ton of flavor, thanks to a simple homemade blackening rub made with basic spices. Roasted zucchini noodles round out the meal. This recipe makes a medium-spicy blackening rub—increase the cayenne or leave it out completely to suit your taste. **Serves 4**

2 tablespoons paprika

1 teaspoon Celtic sea salt or kosher salt, plus more for seasoning

1 teaspoon onion powder

1 teaspoon garlic powder

1 teaspoon dried parsley

¼ teaspoon cayenne pepper

4 (4-ounce) tilapia fillets

Olive oil cooking spray, for preparing the fish

1 pound zucchini noodles

1 tablespoon extra-virgin olive oil

Freshly ground black pepper

1 lemon, cut into wedges

1. Preheat the oven to 400°F.

2. In a small bowl, stir together the paprika, salt, onion powder, garlic powder, parsley, and cayenne. Place the tilapia fillets on one side of a sheet pan. Coat them with cooking spray and rub each with the blackening rub.

3. Spread the zucchini noodles on the other side of the pan. Drizzle with the olive oil.

4. Bake for 12 to 15 minutes, or until the tilapia is cooked through (it will be opaque and flake easily with a fork).

5. Season the zucchini noodles to taste with salt and pepper. Serve the tilapia on top of the zucchini, with the lemon wedges on the side for squeezing.

Preparation tip: Don't add salt to the zucchini before cooking it—it will draw the moisture out and make it soggy.

Per Serving: Calories: 158; Total Fat: 5g; Saturated Fat: 1g; Protein: 23g; Total Carbs: 7g; Fiber: 3g; Net Carbs: 4g; Cholesterol: 55g

DAIRY-FREE, GLUTEN-FREE, NUT-FREE

Chapter 7

DESERTS

BLUEBERRY CRISP

Prep time: 10 minutes / **Cook time:** 45 minutes to 1 hour

Nothing says summer like a fresh fruit crisp. They always remind me of lazy afternoons spent at a pick-your-own orchard, even if the berries are from the grocery store. There's no need to get complicated here—this is the time to let the fruit's flavor really shine—but I can't resist adding a pinch of cinnamon because it tastes so great with the crumbly oat topping. **Serves 6**

2 pints fresh blueberries

2 tablespoons honey

1 tablespoon cornstarch

1 teaspoon ground cinnamon

Juice of 1 lemon

⅓ cup all-purpose flour

⅓ cup packed light
    brown sugar

¼ cup rolled oats

½ teaspoon baking powder

2 tablespoons coconut oil

1. Preheat the oven to 375°F.

2. In a Dutch oven, combine the blueberries, honey, cornstarch, cinnamon, and lemon juice.

3. In a medium bowl, combine the flour, brown sugar, oats, baking powder, and coconut oil. Mix until crumbly. Scatter the crumble over the berries.

4. Bake for 45 minutes to 1 hour until the berries are bubbling and the crumble is crisp and golden brown. Let cool for 15 minutes before serving.

Substitution tip: Use your favorite in-season fruit for this recipe. I have a preference for blueberries, but it's also great with apples or strawberries.

Per Serving: Calories: 230; Total Fat: 5g; Saturated Fat: 4g; Protein: 2g; Total Carbs: 47g; Fiber: 4g; Net Carbs: 43g; Cholesterol: 0mg

DAIRY-FREE, VEGETARIAN

PUMPKIN PIE RICE PUDDING

Prep time: 5 minutes / **Cook time:** 25 minutes

If you ask me, rice pudding is seriously underrated. It's delicious even in its simplest forms, but this pumpkin pie version is far improved. Pumpkin pie spice, a combination of cinnamon, ginger, nutmeg, and cloves, gives it a cozy, warm holiday feel, and pumpkin purée makes it thick and hearty. Serve it plain, or top it with a dollop of whipped cream and a dusting of cinnamon for a real treat. *Serves 6*

½ cup long-grain white rice

2 cups water

1 cup fat-free evaporated milk

½ cup pumpkin purée

¼ cup sugar

¼ cup maple syrup

1 teaspoon pumpkin pie spice

½ teaspoon Celtic sea salt or kosher salt

1. In a Dutch oven over high heat, combine the rice and water. Cook for about 15 minutes until the rice is nearly cooked and the water is evaporated.

2. Stir in the milk, pumpkin purée, sugar, maple syrup, pumpkin pie spice, and salt. Cook for 7 to 10 minutes, stirring constantly, until thickened.

3. Serve chilled.

Ingredient tip: Stir leftover pumpkin purée into your oatmeal or use it in a smoothie.

Per Serving: Calories: 186; Total Fat: 3g; Saturated Fat: 2g; Protein: 4g; Total Carbs: 36g; Fiber: 1g; Net Carbs: 35g; Cholesterol: 12g

GLUTEN-FREE, NUT-FREE, VEGETARIAN

PEACH COBBLER

Prep time: 15 minutes / **Cook time:** 4 hours

Peach cobblers can vary a lot depending on the recipe. Some are more like cake, with peaches intermingled in a soft, sweet batter. My favorite version features syrupy stewed peaches topped with fluffy, lightly sweet biscuits. I love making this for dessert, but it's also a great addition to a brunch. **Serves 6**

Nonstick cooking spray, for preparing the slow cooker

5 fresh peaches, peeled and sliced

¼ cup honey

1 tablespoon cornstarch

½ teaspoon ground cinnamon

½ teaspoon ground ginger

1¼ cups all-purpose flour

3 tablespoons sugar

1 teaspoon baking powder

Pinch Celtic sea salt or kosher salt

4 tablespoons cold unsalted butter

¾ cup milk, or nondairy milk

1. Coat your slow cooker with cooking spray. In the cooker, combine the peaches, honey, cornstarch, cinnamon, and ginger. Mix well.

2. In a medium bowl, combine the flour, sugar, baking powder, and salt. Grate in the butter. Gently mix to form a crumbly mixture. Stir in the milk to form a wet dough. Drop spoonfuls of dough over the peaches.

3. Cover the cooker with a paper towel to trap condensation, cover the paper towel with the lid, and set the cooker to high heat. Cook for 4 hours until the fruit is soft and the biscuits are fluffy.

Substitution tip: I love the set-it-and-forget-it nature of making this in a slow cooker, but you can also make it in the oven. Layer everything in a Dutch oven and bake, uncovered, at 400°F for 30 to 40 minutes until golden brown.

Per Serving: Calories: 299; Total Fat: 9g; Saturated Fat: 5g; Protein: 5g; Total Carbs: 53g; Fiber: 3g; Net Carbs: 50g; Cholesterol: 23mg

NUT-FREE, VEGETARIAN

CHOCOLATE ZUCCHINI CAKE

Prep time: 10 minutes / **Cook time:** 25 minutes

Adding zucchini to cake might seem crazy but, just as in zucchini bread, you'll barely notice it's there. What you will notice is that your cake is extra light and moist, with a great bittersweet chocolate flavor that's just sweet enough without being too sugary. This cake is great for snacking on with a mug of tea or a cup of coffee. A dusting of powdered sugar over the top looks pretty if you need to dress it up for company.

Serves 6

8 tablespoons (1 stick)
　　unsalted butter

⅓ cup sugar

⅓ cup maple syrup

1 teaspoon vanilla extract

¼ cup unsweetened
　　cocoa powder

2 large eggs

½ cup white whole-wheat flour

½ cup almond flour

½ teaspoon baking powder

¼ teaspoon Celtic sea salt or
　　kosher salt

2 cups finely
　　shredded zucchini

1. Preheat the oven to 350°F.

2. In a 9-inch skillet over medium heat, melt the butter. Remove the skillet from the heat and stir in the sugar, maple syrup, vanilla, and cocoa powder. Let cool slightly, about 5 minutes.

3. Whisk in the eggs.

4. Stir in the whole-wheat and almond flours, baking powder, and salt. Fold in the zucchini.

5. Bake for 18 to 20 minutes until the center is set and a toothpick inserted into the middle of the cake comes out clean.

6. Let the cake cool completely. Turn the cake out onto a cutting board and cut it into 6 wedges to serve.

Ingredient tip: Substitute ½ cup of coconut oil for the butter, if you prefer.

Per Serving: Calories: 286; Total Fat: 19g; Saturated Fat: 11g; Protein: 4g; Total Carbs: 29g; Fiber: 3g; Net Carbs: 26g; Cholesterol: 103mg

VEGETARIAN

CRANBERRY OATMEAL BARS

Prep time: 10 minutes / **Cook time:** 25 minutes

I'm obsessed with these cranberry bars. The crumbly oat topping is buttery and sweet, which balances the tart berries perfectly. These bars are crisp straight from the oven, but will soften overnight if kept in an airtight container. Either way, they're fantastic. If you're anything like me, you'll be tempted to sneak one for breakfast. **Serves 6**

½ cup coconut oil

¾ cup maple syrup

1 teaspoon vanilla extract

1½ cups rolled oats

1½ cups white whole-wheat flour

1 teaspoon Celtic sea salt

½ teaspoon ground cinnamon

½ teaspoon baking soda

3 cups fresh cranberries, chopped

1 tablespoon sugar

2 tablespoons sliced almonds

1. Preheat the oven to 350°F.

2. In a large bowl, whisk the coconut oil and maple syrup until smooth. Stir in the vanilla.

3. Gently mix in the oats, flour, salt, cinnamon, and baking soda to form a crumbly dough. Press half the dough onto one side of a sheet pan, forming a layer about ½ inch thick.

4. Spread the chopped cranberries over the dough and sprinkle with the sugar.

5. Crumble the remaining dough over the berries. Sprinkle the top with the almonds.

6. Bake for 22 to 25 minutes until light golden brown.

7. Remove from the oven and let cool completely. Cut into 6 bars to serve.

Ingredient tip: If fresh cranberries aren't in season, use frozen. Or, swap them for whole-fruit raspberry preserves and omit the sugar.

Per Serving: Calories: 373; Total Fat: 20g; Saturated Fat: 16g; Protein: 3g; Total Carbs: 46g; Fiber: 5g; Net Carbs: 41g; Cholesterol: 0mg

DAIRY-FREE, VEGAN, VEGETARIAN

BANANA DONUT HOLES

Prep time: 10 minutes / **Cook time:** 8 minutes

One year, a few blogging friends and I decided to do a whole week of donut recipes the first week in January—diets be damned. Of course, I made sure my contributions had a healthy twist. I love the flavor that mashed bananas give these donut holes, and the air fryer gets them nice and crispy without deep-frying. The dough is too soft to hold its shape in the fryer, so they'll look a little wonky, but, after one bite, you won't care.

Serves 4

1 cup white whole-wheat flour

2 tablespoons granulated sugar

¼ teaspoon baking powder

Dash Celtic sea salt or kosher salt

2 ripe bananas, mashed

2 tablespoons milk, or nondairy milk

¼ teaspoon vanilla extract

Nonstick cooking spray

1 tablespoon cinnamon sugar

1. In a large bowl, stir together the flour, granulated sugar, baking powder, and salt.

2. Stir in the bananas, milk, and vanilla to form a thick, smooth dough.

3. Coat your air fryer's basket with cooking spray. Drop rounded tablespoons of dough into the basket, leaving room between each donut for the air to circulate. Spray the donut holes with cooking spray. Fry at 360°F for 6 to 8 minutes until golden brown and crisp.

4. Sprinkle the donuts with the cinnamon sugar. Let cool for 5 minutes before serving, as the donuts will be very hot inside.

Substitution tip: Switch up these donut holes by swapping the vanilla for coconut extract and adding cardamom or ginger to the cinnamon sugar.

Per Serving: Calories: 203; Total Fat: 3g; Saturated Fat: 2g; Protein: 8g; Total Carbs: 36g; Fiber: 1g; Net Carbs: 35g; Cholesterol: 11mg

NUT-FREE, VEGETARIAN

APPLE & MIXED BERRY GALETTE

Prep time: 10 minutes / **Cook time:** 30 minutes

If you love pie but hate making it, galettes are the answer. They're rustic, freeform pies baked on a sheet pan—and there's no stress because they're not supposed to look perfect anyway. I filled this galette with apple, strawberries, and blueberries—my husband's favorite pie filling. A light coating of flaxseed meal over the crust keeps it from getting soggy and gives it a subtle nutty flavor. **Serves 8**

Nonstick cooking spray, for preparing the sheet pan

1 refrigerated piecrust

1 tablespoon flaxseed meal

1 apple, cored and thinly sliced

1 cup fresh blueberries

1 cup sliced fresh strawberries

2 tablespoons sugar

1 tablespoon lemon zest

¼ teaspoon Celtic sea salt or kosher salt

1 large egg

1 tablespoon water

1. Preheat the oven to 450°F. Coat a sheet pan with cooking spray.

2. Center the piecrust on the prepared sheet pan. Sprinkle it with the flaxseed meal.

3. In a small bowl, stir together the apple, blueberries, strawberries, sugar, lemon zest, and salt. Pour the filling into the center of the piecrust, leaving a 1-inch border around the edge. Fold the edge of the dough up and over the fruit.

4. In the bowl you used for the filling, whisk the egg and water. Brush the egg wash over the crust.

5. Bake the galette for 25 to 30 minutes until the crust is golden brown and the filling is bubbly. Let cool before serving.

Substitution tip: You can swap out the apples and berries for your favorite pie filling combination. Try using all apples, or even make a savory galette filled with Ratatouille (page 125).

Per Serving: Calories: 137; Total Fat: 6g; Saturated Fat: 1g; Protein: 2g; Total Carbs: 19g; Fiber: 2g; Net Carbs: 17g; Cholesterol: 23mg

DAIRY-FREE, NUT-FREE, VEGETARIAN

OATMEAL-CHOCOLATE CHIP COOKIES

Prep time: 15 minutes / **Cook time:** 15 minutes

If you ask me, nothing beats a fresh-from-the-oven cookie. This recipe makes just 6 cookies, so you aren't stuck in the kitchen baking tray after tray, and there aren't a ton of leftovers to tempt you. Coconut oil and shredded coconut keep these cookies super soft, while chocolate chips add to the sweetness. *Serves 6*

2 tablespoons coconut oil

2 tablespoons packed light brown sugar

1 large egg white

¼ teaspoon vanilla extract

¼ cup white whole-wheat flour

½ teaspoon baking powder

Pinch Celtic sea salt or kosher salt

¾ cup rolled oats

¼ cup dark chocolate chips

¼ cup unsweetened shredded coconut

1. Preheat the oven to 350°F. Line a sheet pan with parchment paper.

2. In a large bowl, cream together the coconut oil and brown sugar.

3. Whisk in the egg white and vanilla.

4. Stir in the flour, baking powder, and salt to form a thin dough. Stir in the oats, chocolate chips, and coconut. Drop rounded tablespoons of dough onto the prepared sheet pan.

5. Bake for 14 to 16 minutes until the centers are set and the edges are golden brown. Let the cookies cool for at least 5 minutes before removing from the sheet pan.

Make-ahead tip: Double this recipe, form the cookies, and freeze half to bake another time! If baking the cookies frozen, they'll take an extra 2 to 3 minutes in the oven.

Per Serving: Calories: 199; Total Fat: 12g; Saturated Fat: 10g; Protein: 4g; Total Carbs: 21g; Fiber: 3g; Net Carbs: 18g; Cholesterol: 0mg

DAIRY-FREE, VEGETARIAN

Chapter 8

SNACKS & SIDES

CRISPY SALT & VINEGAR CHICKPEAS

Prep time: 5 minutes / **Cook time:** 15 minutes

Roasted chickpeas are one of my favorite snacks. You can make them in the oven, but they come out even better when you make them in an air fryer. They're crispy outside, creamy inside, and you can change the seasonings to match your mood. These salt-and-vinegar chickpeas have a subtle flavor so they're perfect for snacking, but you can also use them to add crunch to soups, salads, or grain bowls. **Serves 6**

1 (15-ounce) can low-sodium chickpeas, drained

1 tablespoon malt vinegar or distilled white vinegar

½ teaspoon extra-virgin olive oil

½ teaspoon Celtic sea salt

1. In a small bowl, stir together the chickpeas, vinegar, olive oil, and salt. Mix well. Transfer the chickpeas to your air fryer's basket. Fry at 370°F for 15 minutes, shaking the basket halfway through the cooking time.

2. Let the chickpeas cool in a single layer. They will continue to crisp as they cool.

3. To store, drain, as needed. Refrigerate, covered, for 3 to 5 days, or freeze for up to 3 months.

Preparation tip: If you don't have an air fryer, roast the chickpeas on a sheet pan in a 450°F oven for 30 minutes, stirring halfway through the cooking time.

Per Serving: Calories: 99; Total Fat: 1g; Saturated Fat: 0g; Protein: 4g; Total Carbs: 18g; Fiber: 4g; Net Carbs: 14g; Cholesterol: 0mg

DAIRY-FREE, NUT-FREE, VEGAN, VEGETARIAN

BABA GHANOUSH

Prep time: 10 minutes / **Cook time:** 10 minutes

Baba ghanoush is a dip that's similar to hummus, but made with roasted eggplant instead of chickpeas. Whoever invented it is a genius—eggplant gives the dip a silky texture and mildly floral flavor. Traditional recipes use eggplant that has been smoked on a grill, but I get a similar effect by broiling mine in the oven. Use this as a dip for pita chips or raw veggies, or try it as a sandwich spread. *Serves 6*

1 large (about 1 pound) globe eggplant, cut into ½-inch-thick rounds

2 tablespoons tahini

2 garlic cloves, peeled

Juice of 1 lemon

¼ cup fresh cilantro or parsley

1 teaspoon Celtic sea salt

Pinch ground cumin

1 teaspoon extra-virgin olive oil

1. Preheat the broiler.

2. Place the eggplant rounds on a sheet pan. Broil for 10 minutes until soft and golden brown. Scoop the eggplant into a blender, discarding the skin.

3. Add the tahini, garlic, lemon juice, cilantro, salt, and cumin. Blend into a thick paste. Scrape the dip into a bowl and drizzle with the olive oil. Cover and refrigerate until ready to serve. The baba ghanoush will keep, refrigerated, for 3 to 5 days.

Ingredient tip: Tahini is a paste made from toasted, ground sesame seeds. Look for it near the condiments or near other Middle Eastern foods.

Per Serving: Calories: 64; Total Fat: 4g; Saturated Fat: 1g; Protein: 2g; Total Carbs: 7g; Fiber: 4g; Net Carbs: 3g; Cholesterol: 0mg

DAIRY-FREE, GLUTEN-FREE, NUT-FREE, VEGAN, VEGETARIAN

QUICK PICKLES

Prep time: 5 minutes / **Cook time:** 5 minutes

I love pickles! This basic recipe works on pretty much any vegetable—from cucumbers to green beans. You can use the pickles right away, but the flavor gets even better after they've been refrigerated for a night or two. Enjoy them as a snack, or add pickled cucumbers to your pulled pork, or top your tacos and chili with pickled red onions. **Serves 6**

1 cup thinly sliced vegetable of choice

2 garlic cloves, smashed

½ cup apple cider vinegar

1 teaspoon honey

Pinch Celtic sea salt or kosher salt

1. Place the vegetables and garlic in a heat-proof container.

2. In a small skillet over medium-high heat, combine the vinegar, honey, and salt. Bring to a boil. Remove the liquid from the heat and pour it over the vegetables.

3. Let the pickles cool to room temperature. Eat immediately, or refrigerate, covered, for up to 2 months.

Ingredient tip: This all-purpose recipe is pretty basic. Depending on what vegetable you're using, add other herbs or spices such as dill or whole coriander seeds.

Per Serving: Calories: 12; Total Fat: 0g; Saturated Fat: 0g; Protein: 0g; Total Carbs: 2g; Fiber: 0g; Net Carbs: 2g; Cholesterol: 0mg

DAIRY-FREE, GLUTEN-FREE, NUT-FREE, VEGETARIAN

SLOW COOKER BAKED POTATOES

Prep time: 5 minutes / **Cook time:** 8 hours

Baked potatoes are a great side dish, but I'm too impatient to make them in the oven. Luckily, they come out perfectly in the slow cooker. I stick a few in there in the morning, and my potatoes are perfectly soft and fluffy when I get home from work. If you're making them ahead, be sure to let the potatoes cool to room temperature before refrigerating or the skin will get super soggy from condensation. **Serves 4**

4 russet potatoes, pierced all over with the tines of a fork

Place the potatoes in your slow cooker. Cover the cooker and set it to low heat. Cook for 8 hours.

Repurpose tip: Baked potatoes are great on the side of meats and veggies, or top them with chili or air-fried broccoli and a little Cheddar cheese.

Per Serving: Calories: 168; Total Fat: 0g; Saturated Fat: 0g; Protein: 5g; Total Carbs: 38g; Fiber: 3g; Net Carbs: 35g; Cholesterol: 0g

DAIRY-FREE, GLUTEN-FREE, NUT-FREE, VEGAN, VEGETARIAN

PRESSURE COOKER BROWN RICE

Prep time: 5 minutes / **Time to pressure:** 5 minutes / **Cook time:** 15 minutes / **Release time:** 5 minutes

Cauliflower rice is great because it cooks so quickly, but sometimes you want the real deal. Using a pressure cooker cuts the cooking time for brown rice by about half and it comes out so fluffy. Leftover rice can dry out, but it's perfect to use in a stir-fry. You can also add a few tablespoons of water to the pan as you reheat it to soften it up.

Serves 6

1 cup long-grain brown rice

1 cup Garden Vegetable Stock (page 135) or Chicken Stock (page 133), or low-sodium store-bought vegetable or chicken stock

1. In your pressure cooker, combine the rice and stock. Lock the lid in place and set the cooker to High pressure for 15 minutes.

2. When the cook time ends, manually release the pressure.

Substitution tip: I like to cook my rice in vegetable or chicken stock for extra flavor, but you can also use water.

Per Serving: Calories: 116; Total Fat: 1g; Saturated Fat: 0g; Protein: 2g; Total Carbs: 24g; Fiber: 2g; Net Carbs: 22g; Cholesterol: 0g

DAIRY-FREE, GLUTEN-FREE, NUT-FREE, VEGAN, VEGETARIAN

RATATOUILLE

Prep time: 10 minutes / **Cook time:** 40 minutes

Ratatouille is a delicious French vegetable stew made with eggplant, zucchini, fennel, and just enough tomato to make it a little saucy. It's great as a side dish, but you can also use it to bulk up an omelet or top a pizza. Also try it in a wrap with Baba Ghanoush (page 121) and feta for a great Mediterranean-inspired meal. **Serves 6**

1 zucchini, diced

1 eggplant, peeled and diced

1 red bell pepper, thinly sliced

1 fennel bulb, cored, stalks
  removed, bulb thinly sliced

1 tomato, diced

4 garlic cloves, minced

2 tablespoons extra-virgin
  olive oil

¼ teaspoon dried thyme

¼ teaspoon dried oregano

¼ cup fresh basil, chopped

Celtic sea salt or kosher salt

Freshly ground black pepper

1. Preheat the oven to 350°F.

2. In a Dutch oven, combine the zucchini, eggplant, red bell pepper, fennel, tomato, garlic, olive oil, thyme, and oregano. Mix well. Cover the pot and bake for 40 minutes until the vegetables are soft.

3. Remove from the oven and stir in the basil. Season to taste with salt and pepper.

Ingredient tip: Fennel is a vegetable with a texture similar to celery and a licorice-like flavor. You can leave it out, if you prefer, but it gives this recipe its characteristically French flavor.

Per Serving: Calories: 88; Total Fat: 5g; Saturated Fat: 1g; Protein: 2g; Total Carbs: 11g; Fiber: 5g; Net Carbs: 6g; Cholesterol: 0mg

DAIRY-FREE, GLUTEN-FREE, NUT-FREE, VEGAN, VEGETARIAN

ROASTED BRUSSELS SPROUTS WITH BACON & PECANS

Prep time: 10 minutes / **Cook time:** 35 minutes

Crispy roasted Brussels sprouts are one of my favorite winter vegetables. This recipe gets an upgrade from crispy bacon and sweet shallot. A splash of vinegar stirred in at the end brightens everything. This recipe is perfect for winter holidays—make a double batch because they go fast! **Serves 5**

1 pound Brussels sprouts, halved

4 sugar-free bacon slices, chopped

2 shallots, thinly sliced

1 teaspoon extra-virgin olive oil

Celtic sea salt or kosher salt

Freshly ground black pepper

¼ cup chopped pecans

1 tablespoon balsamic vinegar

1. Preheat the oven to 400°F.

2. Place the Brussels sprouts, bacon, and shallots on a rimmed sheet pan. Drizzle with the olive oil and season generously with salt and pepper. Toss to coat.

3. Roast for 35 minutes until the Brussels sprouts are tender. Stir in the pecans and vinegar.

Substitution tip: Pecans can be expensive, but you can usually find smaller bags in the baking aisle. You can also substitute walnuts or omit the nuts.

Per Serving: Calories: 143; Total Fat: 9g; Saturated Fat: 2g; Protein: 9g; Total Carbs: 9g; Fiber: 4g; Net Carbs: 5g; Cholesterol: 17mg

DAIRY-FREE, GLUTEN-FREE

AIR-FRIED BUFFALO CAULIFLOWER

Prep time: 5 minutes / **Cook time:** 20 minutes

This air-fried Buffalo cauliflower is a lighter take on those wings that are practically a staple in upstate New York. A light coating of bread crumbs ensures they're nice and crispy, and adding the sauce before they're cooked makes them less messy to eat. If you like saucier "wings," toss them in another ¼ cup of sauce when they come out of the fryer. **Serves 6**

1½ cups cauliflower florets

¼ cup wing sauce

¼ cup plain bread crumbs

1. In a large bowl, combine the cauliflower and wing sauce. Stir to coat.

2. Sprinkle with the bread crumbs and gently stir to combine. Arrange the cauliflower in a single layer in your air fryer's basket. Fry at 320°F for 20 minutes. Serve hot.

Substitution tip: Wing sauce is a combination of hot sauce and butter, so it's not as spicy as pure hot sauce. You can make your own at home by mixing ⅔ cup of hot sauce with ¼ cup of melted butter. Cover and refrigerate any leftovers for about 2 weeks.

Per Serving: Calories: 26; Total Fat: 0g; Saturated Fat: 0g; Protein: 1g; Total Carbs: 5g; Fiber: 1g; Net Carbs: 4g; Cholesterol: 0mg

NUT-FREE, VEGETARIAN

Chapter 9

STAPLES & SAUCES

SUPER SIMPLE MARINARA

Prep time: 5 minutes / **Cook time:** 1 hour

Marinara is great for throwing together a quick pot of pasta or topping pizza or chicken Parmesan. I always have some in my refrigerator, and I keep a backup in the freezer. Jarred pasta sauce can be full of hidden sugar and salt, but this homemade marinara is simple and you control what's in it—plus your kitchen will smell so good while it cooks! **Makes 6 cups**

2 tablespoons extra-virgin olive oil

1 onion, finely diced

8 garlic cloves, minced

2 (28-ounce) cans no-salt-added crushed tomatoes

2 tablespoons tomato paste

2 teaspoons dried oregano

2 teaspoons dried parsley

1. In a Dutch oven over medium heat, heat the olive oil.

2. Add the onion and garlic. Cook for 5 minutes, or until softened.

3. Add the tomatoes, tomato paste, oregano, and parsley. Stir to combine. Bring to a simmer and turn the heat to low. Simmer for 1 hour to thicken. For a smoother texture, purée the sauce using an immersion blender, or in a standard blender. If not using immediately, refrigerate in an airtight container for up to 3 to 4 days, or freeze for up to 6 months.

Repurpose tip: Add Kalamata olives, capers, and red pepper flakes to turn this simple marinara into a zesty puttanesca.

Per Serving (½ cup): Calories: 86; Total Fat: 5g; Saturated Fat: 1g; Protein: 1g; Total Carbs: 8g; Fiber: 1g; Net Carbs: 7g; Cholesterol: 0g

DAIRY-FREE, GLUTEN-FREE, NUT-FREE, VEGAN, VEGETARIAN

CHICKEN STOCK

Prep time: 5 minutes / **Time to pressure:** 15 minutes / **Cook time:** 25 minutes / **Release time:** 7 minutes

I haven't found a store-bought chicken stock that comes anywhere close to home-made stock in terms of flavor. Luckily, it's super easy to make at home and, when you use your pressure cooker, it only takes about 1 hour. **Makes 1 gallon**

1 tablespoon extra-virgin olive oil

4 carrots, roughly chopped

4 celery stalks, roughly chopped

1 onion, roughly chopped

4 garlic cloves, peeled

2 pounds bone-in, skin-on chicken thighs or drumsticks

2 bay leaves

3 quarts water

1. On your pressure cooker, select Sauté. Pour in the olive oil to heat.

2. Add the carrots, celery, onion, and garlic. Sauté for 5 minutes.

3. Add the chicken, bay leaves, and water. Lock the lid in place and set the cooker to High pressure for 20 minutes.

4. When the cook time ends, let the pressure release naturally.

5. Strain the broth, discarding any solid pieces. Keep refrigerated in an airtight container for 3 to 4 days, or freeze for up to 6 months.

Ingredient tip: Don't discard the chicken after it's cooked. Shred it to use in soup or add to burrito bowls.

Per Serving (1 cup): Calories: 43; Total Fat: 1g; Saturated Fat: 0g; Protein: 3g; Total Carbs: 3g; Fiber: 1g; Net Carbs: 2g; Cholesterol: 4mg

DAIRY-FREE, GLUTEN-FREE, NUT-FREE

GARDEN VEGETABLE STOCK

Prep time: 10 minutes / **Time to pressure:** 15 minutes / **Cook time:** 30 minutes / **Release time:** 15 minutes

Store-bought vegetable stock can be somewhat of a gamble—some are super tomato-y and can make everything taste like minestrone. This stock gets its flavor from mushrooms and zucchini, so it has a more neutral flavor and golden, chicken-like color that work in almost any recipe. **Makes 3 quarts**

4 ounces sliced
  white mushrooms

3 carrots, roughly chopped

2 celery stalks,
  roughly chopped

1 onion, roughly chopped

1 zucchini, roughly chopped

4 thyme sprigs

2 garlic cloves, peeled

2 bay leaves

3 quarts water

1. In your pressure cooker, combine the mushrooms, carrots, celery, onion, zucchini, thyme, garlic, bay leaves, and water. Lock the lid in place and set the cooker to High pressure for 30 minutes.

2. When the cook time ends, let the pressure release naturally.

3. Strain and discard any solid pieces. Keep refrigerated in an airtight container for 3 to 4 days, or freeze for up to 6 months.

Ingredient tip: I usually use cremini mushrooms, but, in this recipe, white mushrooms give the stock a milder, less earthy flavor and a clear color.

Per Serving (1 cup): Calories: 15; Total Fat: 0g; Saturated Fat: 0g; Protein: 0g; Total Carbs: 3g; Fiber: 0g; Net Carbs: 3g; Cholesterol: 0mg

DAIRY-FREE, GLUTEN-FREE, NUT-FREE, VEGAN, VEGETARIAN

MAPLE BARBECUE SAUCE

Prep time: 5 minutes / **Cook time:** 15 minutes

Homemade barbecue sauce is incredibly easy to make, and I love that I control the sugar and sweeten it with maple syrup. I also love barbecue with a kick, so I always add a few splashes of habanero hot sauce to mine. This is great on anything from chicken to salmon, or used as a dip for roasted potato wedges. *Makes 3 cups*

1 tablespoon extra-virgin olive oil

1 red onion, minced

4 garlic cloves, minced

2 cups ketchup, preferably unsweetened

½ cup maple syrup

½ cup apple cider vinegar

1 tablespoon Dijon mustard

¼ to ½ teaspoon hot sauce (optional)

1. In an 8-inch skillet over medium heat, heat the olive oil.

2. Add the red onion and garlic. Sauté for 5 minutes.

3. Stir in the ketchup, maple syrup, vinegar, mustard, and hot sauce (if using). Bring to a simmer and cook for 10 minutes until thickened. Keep refrigerated in an airtight container for up to 1 week.

Ingredient tip: Ketchup can be loaded with added sugar and corn syrup, but you can find unsweetened options. Look for one with no sugar added, as the honey- and date-sweetened versions have a different flavor.

Per Serving (2 tablespoons): Calories: 46; Total Fat: 1g; Saturated Fat: 0g; Protein: 1g; Total Carbs: 10g; Fiber: 0g; Net Carbs: 10g; Cholesterol: 0mg

DAIRY-FREE, GLUTEN-FREE, NUT-FREE, VEGAN, VEGETARIAN

ALL-PURPOSE GREEK DRESSING

Prep time: 5 minutes

This is my go-to salad dressing for everything, and I always keep a jar of it in the refrigerator. Use it on green salads, as a marinade for chicken or pork, or mix it with Greek yogurt and use it as a dressing for a new twist on chicken salad. The dressing will separate as it sits, so give it a good shake before you use it. **Makes 1¼ cups**

1 cup red wine vinegar
Juice of 2 lemons
8 garlic cloves, minced
1 tablespoon dried oregano
¼ cup extra-virgin olive oil
Celtic sea salt or kosher salt
Freshly ground black pepper

In a small bowl, whisk the vinegar, lemon juice, garlic, and oregano. Slowly whisk in the olive oil. Season to taste with salt and pepper. Keep refrigerated in an airtight container for up to 1 week.

Substitution tip: If you don't need this recipe to be vegan, omit the salt and add 1 tablespoon each of feta brine and peperoncini brine. It adds a complex, spicy flavor to the dressing that takes it to the next level.

Per Serving (2 tablespoons): Calories: 55; Total Fat: 5g; Saturated Fat: 1g; Protein: 0g; Total Carbs: 2g; Fiber: 0g; Net Carbs: 2g; Cholesterol: 0mg

DAIRY-FREE, GLUTEN-FREE, NUT-FREE, VEGETARIAN, VEGAN

PRESSURE-COOKED HARD-BOILED EGGS

Prep time: 5 minutes / **Time to pressure:** 5 minutes / **Cook time:** 5 minutes / **Release time:** 5 minutes

Hard-boiled eggs are really useful to have around and they'll keep in the refrigerator for about a week. Add them to salads or ramen, or use them as a grab-and-go break-fast option. You can even reheat them and serve them with Butternut Squash Hash (see page 24). **Serves 6**

1 cup water
6 large eggs

1. Place a wire rack in the bottom of your pressure cooker. Pour in the water. Place the eggs on top of the rack. Lock the lid in place and set the cooker to High pressure for 5 minutes.

2. When the cook time ends, let the pressure release naturally for 5 minutes; quick release any remaining pressure.

3. Run the eggs under cold water until they're cool to the touch. Peel immediately. Cover leftover eggs with a damp paper towel and refrigerate for up to 1 week.

Leftovers tip: Use this technique to make as many or as few eggs as you want; just make sure they fit in a single layer.

Per Serving: Calories: 72; Total Fat: 5g; Saturated Fat: 2g; Protein: 6g; Total Carbs: 0g; Fiber: 0g; Net Carbs: 0g; Cholesterol: 186mg

DAIRY-FREE, GLUTEN-FREE, NUT-FREE, VEGETARIAN

HOMEMADE ENCHILADA SAUCE

Prep time: 5 minutes / **Cook time:** 5 minutes

Homemade enchilada sauce is quick and easy and the flavor is unmatched. It's the base to my Chicken Enchilada Sweet Potato Noodles (page 56), but it's also great on more traditional enchiladas or with eggs. I use vegetable stock so I can use it in vegan and vegetarian recipes, but chicken stock also works, if you prefer. **Makes 2 cups**

2 cups tomato sauce

½ cup Garden Vegetable Stock (page 135), or low-sodium store-bought vegetable stock

2 tablespoons apple cider vinegar

2 garlic cloves, minced

1 tablespoon gluten-free chili powder

½ teaspoon ground cumin

In a Dutch oven over medium heat, stir together the tomato sauce, vegetable stock, vinegar, garlic, chili powder, and cumin. Bring to a boil. Simmer for 5 minutes until thickened slightly. Keep refrigerated in an airtight container for 3 to 4 days, or freeze for up to 6 months.

Substitution tip: For a deeper, smoky flavor, use chipotle chile powder in place of traditional chili powder.

Per Serving (¼ cup): Calories: 20; Total Fat: 0g; Saturated Fat: 0g; Protein: 1g; Total Carbs: 4g; Fiber: 1g; Net Carbs: 3g; Cholesterol: 0mg

DAIRY-FREE, GLUTEN-FREE, NUT-FREE, VEGAN, VEGETARIAN

CHIMICHURRI SAUCE

Prep time: 10 minutes

Chimichurri is a surprise powerhouse of a condiment. It has a bright flavor that's great on anything from grilled steak to egg sandwiches to pasta. You can also thin it with another tablespoon each of oil and vinegar and use it as a vinaigrette or mix it into Greek yogurt to use as a dressing for potato salad. *Serves 6*

1 small shallot, minced

2 garlic cloves, minced

½ jalapeño pepper, seeded and minced

¼ cup finely chopped fresh cilantro

2 tablespoons finely chopped fresh parsley

1 tablespoon finely chopped fresh oregano leaves

¼ cup red wine vinegar

2 tablespoons extra-virgin olive oil

Celtic sea salt

In a small bowl, combine the shallot, garlic, jalapeño, cilantro, parsley, oregano, vinegar, and olive oil. Season to taste with salt. Stir to combine. Cover and refrigerate until ready to use, or for up to 3 to 4 days.

Substitution tip: If you don't like cilantro, use more parsley instead.

Per Serving: Calories: 48; Total Fat: 5g; Saturated Fat: 1g; Protein: 0g; Total Carbs: 1g; Fiber: 0g; Net Carbs: 1g; Cholesterol: 0mg

DAIRY-FREE, GLUTEN-FREE, NUT-FREE, VEGAN, VEGETARIAN

PIZZA DOUGH

Prep time: 10 minutes / **Inactive time:** 1 hour

I always have a hunk of pizza dough in my refrigerator. Besides using it for pizza, you can bake it into a baguette or dinner rolls, or stuff it with apples and cinnamon for a breakfast treat. I use a mixture of all-purpose flour, whole-wheat flour, and flaxseed meal to add a little extra fiber and a subtly nutty flavor while maintaining the perfect light and fluffy texture. **Serves 8**

1 (¼-ounce) packet instant yeast

1¼ cups lukewarm water

1 tablespoon extra-virgin olive oil

2 cups all-purpose flour

1 cup white whole-wheat flour

1 teaspoon Celtic sea salt or kosher salt

¼ cup flaxseed meal

1. In a large bowl, combine the yeast, water, olive oil, all-purpose and whole-wheat flours, and salt. Mix well to form a soft, sticky dough.

2. Knead in the flaxseed meal. Cover the dough and let rise in a warm place for 1 hour, or until doubled in size.

3. Divide the dough into 2 portions. Wrap each in plastic wrap, refrigerate for up to 1 day, or freeze until ready to use. It will keep, refrigerated, for up to 2 to 3 days, or it can be frozen for up to 6 months.

Ingredient tip: White whole-wheat flour is softer and has a milder flavor than traditional red wheat, making it great for baked goods.

Per Serving: Calories: 195; Total Fat: 4g; Saturated Fat: 1g; Protein: 7g; Total Carbs: 34g; Fiber: 6g; Net Carbs: 28g; Cholesterol: 0mg

DAIRY-FREE, NUT-FREE, VEGAN, VEGETARIAN

PRESSURE COOKER BEANS

Prep time: 5 minutes / **Time to pressure:** 10 minutes / **Cook time:** 25 minutes / **Release time:** 25 minutes

I cook with beans a lot because they're an easy source of lean protein. Buying canned beans gets expensive and they take up a ton of space in my cabinets. A big bag of dried beans, on the other hand, costs about a dollar and they're easy to make in a pressure cooker. I add stock and a bay leaf for extra flavor and season to taste with salt. **Makes 6 cups**

1 pound dried black or
   pinto beans

5 cups water, or Garden
   Vegetable Stock (page 135),
   or low-sodium store-bought
   vegetable stock

1 bay leaf

Celtic sea salt or kosher salt

1. In your pressure cooker, combine the beans, water, and bay leaf. Lock the lid in place and set the cooker to High pressure for 25 minutes. Let the pressure release naturally.

2. Remove and discard the bay leaf. Season the beans to taste with salt. Keep refrigerated in an airtight container for 3 to 4 days, or freeze for up to 6 months.

Leftovers tip: Refrigerate the beans in their cooking liquid to prevent them from drying out.

Per Serving (½ cup): Calories: 129; Total Fat: 1g; Saturated Fat: 0g; Protein: 8g; Total Carbs: 24g; Fiber: 6g; Net Carbs: 18g; Cholesterol: 0mg

DAIRY-FREE, GLUTEN-FREE, NUT-FREE, VEGAN, VEGETARIAN

THE DIRTY DOZEN AND THE CLEAN FIFTEEN™

A nonprofit environmental watchdog organization called Environmental Working Group (EWG) looks at data supplied by the US Department of Agriculture (USDA) and the Food and Drug Administration (FDA) about pesticide residues. Each year it compiles a list of the best and worst pesticide loads found in commercial crops. You can use these lists to decide which fruits and vegetables to buy organic to minimize your exposure to pesticides and which produce is considered safe enough to buy conventionally. This does not mean they are pesticide-free, though, so wash these fruits and vegetables thoroughly.

Dirty Dozen™

apples	strawberries
celery	sweet bell peppers
cherries	tomatoes
grapes	
nectarines	
peaches	
pears	
potatoes	
spinach	

Additionally, nearly three-quarters of hot pepper samples contained pesticide residues

Clean Fifteen™

asparagus	kiwis
avocados	mangos
broccoli	onions
cabbages	papayas
cantaloupes	pineapples
cauliflower	sweet corn
eggplants	sweet peas (frozen)
honeydew melons	

MEASUREMENT CONVERSIONS

Volume Equivalents (Liquid)

US Standard	US Standard (ounces)	Metric (approximate)
2 tablespoons	1 fl. oz.	30 mL
¼ cup	2 fl. oz.	60 mL
½ cup	4 fl. oz.	120 mL
1 cup	8 fl. oz.	240 mL
1½ cups	12 fl. oz.	355 mL
2 cups or 1 pint	16 fl. oz.	475 mL
4 cups or 1 quart	32 fl. oz.	1 L
1 gallon	128 fl. oz.	4 L

Oven Temperatures

Fahrenheit	Celsius (approximate)
250°F	120°C
300°F	150°C
325°F	165°C
350°F	180°C
375°F	190°C
400°F	200°C
425°F	220°C
450°F	230°C

Volume Equivalents (Dry)

US Standard	Metric (approximate)
⅛ teaspoon	0.5 mL
¼ teaspoon	1 mL
½ teaspoon	2 mL
¾ teaspoon	4 mL
1 teaspoon	5 mL
1 tablespoon	15 mL
¼ cup	59 mL
⅓ cup	79 mL
½ cup	118 mL
⅔ cup	156 mL
¾ cup	177 mL
1 cup	235 mL
2 cups or 1 pint	475 mL
3 cups	700 mL
4 cups or 1 quart	1 L

Weight Equivalents

US Standard	Metric (approximate)
½ ounce	15 g
1 ounce	30 g
2 ounces	60 g
4 ounces	115 g
8 ounces	225 g
12 ounces	340 g
16 ounces or 1 pound	455 g

RESOURCES

Kitchen Tools

Chicago Metallic: ChicagoMetallicBakeware.com
Sheet pans
Circulon: Circulon.com
12-inch deep skillet: This skillet is huge—you can fit a ton of food in it—but it's not heavy at all.
Lodge cast iron: LodgeMFG.com
Lodge makes gorgeous, quality products for under $100. I especially love their 7-quart oval oven. They also make great cast iron skillets that can go from stovetop to the oven.
Microplane graters: US.Microplane.com
These are super sharp so the food doesn't stick. I have extra-coarse and fine graters and use both regularly.
OXO: OXO.com
Sheet pans and small kitchen gadgets
Wilton: Wilton.com/shop-cake-pans
A 6-inch baking pan makes your air fryer and pressure cooker so much more versatile. You can buy disposable foil pans, but Wilton makes a sturdy metal pan for under $10.

Ingredients

Bob's Red Mill: BobsRedMill.com
Whole grains
Huy Fong: HuyFong.com
Sambal oelek and chili-garlic sauce
King Arthur Flour: KingArthurFlour.com/shop-home
White whole-wheat flour and gluten-free baking blend
Primal Kitchen: PrimalKitchen.com
Sugar-free ketchup
Tessemae's Dressing: Tessemaes.com
High-quality organic salad dressings
The Spice House: TheSpiceHouse.com
All the gluten-free spices and blends you can imagine

RECIPE INDEX

INDEX

ACKNOWLEDGMENTS

Thank you to my husband, Shawn, for putting up with my nonsense, tasting all my recipes (even when they have tomatoes), and being honest with me even when you know I won't like it. I don't know how I'd get through life without you. I love you so much.

To everyone who has read my blog, *Healthy Delicious*, whether you're a devoted fan or just a passerby. I wouldn't do this if it weren't for your support, enthusiasm, and excitement. Nothing makes me happier than when you tell me one of my recipes is your new favorite.

To the entire blogging community, but especially to Sarah Caron, Samantha Ferraro, and Dani Meyer, thank you for guiding me through this process and encouraging me to keep going when it all seemed overwhelming. You have no idea how much you've helped.

To my FP sparkle sisters, Cait, Dana, Kelly, Kim, Monica, Rosanna, and Stephanie; thank you for your constant support and encouragement. When's our next trip?

Brenna, thank you for always being there when I need to vent and for letting me complain about how exhausted I was when I know you were, too.

Linda and Laura, thanks for encouraging me and not telling me I was crazy to write a book during campaign season (even though I was!).

Mary, sorry I've fallen off the face of the earth while taking on this project. I miss you!

ABOUT THE AUTHOR

LAUREN KEATING is the author behind the blog *Healthy Delicious*, where she has been sharing easy weeknight recipes made with fresh, nutritious ingredients for the last 10 years. She studied plant-based professional cooking through Rouxbe cooking school and uses those skills to incorporate fruits, vegetables, and whole grains into her recipes in unique ways.

She lives in Upstate New York with her husband, Shawn, and their two dogs. This is her first cookbook.

You can read more from Lauren at Healthy-Delicious.com, or find her on Instagram and Twitter @HealthyDelish.